CROSS-STROKES

C R O S S STROKES

Poetry between Los Angeles and San Francisco

EDITED BY

Neeli Cherkovski and Bill Mohr

OTIS BOOKS | SEISMICITY EDITIONS

The Graduate Writing program
Otis College of Art and Design
LOS ANGELES ● 2015

"On Flower Wreath Hill (i-vi)" by Kenneth Rexroth, from *The Morning Star*, © 1979 by Kenneth Rexroth. Reprinted by permission of New Directions Publishing Corp.

"Apollo Sends Seven Nursery Rhymes to James Alexander" by Jack Spicer, © 1959 by the Estate of Jack Spicer.

"Song of the Adoumboulou" (excerpt: section 40, pages 21, 22, 23 and 24) by Nathaniel Mackey, from *Splay Anthem*, © 2002 by Nathaniel Mackey. Reprinted by permission of New Directions Publishing Corp.

Four poems anthologized in *Collected Poems* of Lenore Kandel, published by North Atlantic Books, © 2012 by the Estate of Lenore Kandel, originally published in *Word Alchemy*, published by Grove Press, © 1967 by Lenore Kandel. Reprinted by permission of North Atlantic Books.

Bruce Boyd, "Venice Recalled" appeared in Donald Allen's *New American Poetry*. © Bruce Boyd, 1960.

Every effort has been made to contact the authors and to secure their permission to reprint poems. All interested parties should contact the publisher, with whom appropriate arrangements will be made to satisfy their claims.

Book design and typesetting: Rebecca Chamlee

Second Printing

ISBN: 0-9860173-9-6
ISBN-13: 978-0-9860173-9-1

OTIS BOOKS | SEISMICITY EDITIONS
The Graduate Writing program
Otis College of Art and Design

9045 Lincoln Boulevard
Los Angeles, CA 90045

http://www.otis.edu/graduate-writing/seismicity-editions
seismicity@otis.edu

CONTENTS

Back in 1972, *Anthology of L.A. Poets*, edited by Paul Vangelisti, Charles Bukowski and myself, provided needed focus for the local poetry community. Before that, there had been only a single collection of Los Angeles poets, *Poetry Los Angeles* (1960), but nothing addressing the full diversity of the L.A. scene. While *Anthology of L.A. Poets* was more compact than comprehensive, it drew upon the many interests of its editors. We kicked off the project with a call for submissions from far-flung neighborhoods, and even from places only rumored to exist. The writing stacked up. We sorted through what we had and came up with a song or chorus of what made the city move. Much of the work reflected a loner quality with images of L.A.'s elusive core; at least that's how I remember it.

The anthology, led off by a rambunctious forward by Bukowski, served as proof that poetry actually existed in Los Angeles. So much attention had been given to San Francisco, and the entire Bay Area, due largely to the Berkeley poetry renaissance and the Beat phenomenon, that we had for long felt short-changed. Since the turn of the 20th Century, San Franciscans viewed their southern neighbor with disdain. When I moved to San Francisco, no one I initially met owned a copy of the book I had helped to edit. Even when concrete proof was available, it was easier to ignore Los Angeles than to take it seriously. This attitude was reinforced by other poets who had moved north, almost as if they felt compelled to belittle what they had left behind. Jack Hirschman had migrated a year before me and was already railing against the glitz of Los Angeles. He had been an instructor at UCLA and now was proclaiming himself "a poet of the streets," and decades later would become one of San Francisco's poet laureates. David Meltzer, in a more quiet way, had moved north years earlier to take his place in San Francisco, as had Lenore Kandel. On the other hand, not far from my first apartment in North Beach stood the building where Paul Vangelisti grew up. He had moved south initially to enroll in a Ph.D. program at the University of Southern California, but had decided to commit himself to avant-garde cultural work instead of finishing a dissertation. Along with John McBride in San Francisco, Vangelisti had already launched his magazine, *Invisible City*, by the time he began work on *Anthology of L.A. Poets* with Bukowski and me. That magazine drew much of its strength from the intersection between L.A. and S.F. and was one of the inspirations for *Cross-Strokes*.

I was very happy when I drove north to San Francisco in 1974, my car loaded with books and clothing, and if I felt any homesickness at all, it was easily resolved in my first weeks as a "San Francisco poet." All I had to do was to imagine the lingering presence of John Thomas and Stuart Perkoff, a pair of Venice West poets who had lived and written poetry in this area after first living in Southern California, and both of whom had subsequently returned to Los Angeles. I settled in and began to mature as a poet and chronicler of literary movements in books such as *Whitman's Wild Children*. Even as I finally felt truly at home in San Francisco, however, I never succumbed to the local prejudice. One of my first conversations with Beat icon Lawrence Ferlinghetti, for instance, was about the two cities. He shared that old attitude that L.A. was nothing more than a glorified parking lot.

Cross-Strokes extends the idea of an anthology based on geography. There have been many regional anthologies before, usually centered in major cities, but this one is more rare, more of an oddity. You'd almost have to have spent years either driving or flying up and down California, tooling along highways 5 or 101, landing at LAX or SFO, to have come up with such a landscape of poetry as in *Cross-Strokes*. L.A. is deep noir and its rhythms often take time to appreciate. When I re-visit, I love to begin in the city's Spanish-era plaza and wend my way down a freeway or a long boulevard to get the flavor of the town again. Hollywood, San Fernando Valley, Venice Beach, Watts, the Sunset corridor — a pueblo grown to an immense size, and one in which it is easy to get lost. San Francisco, on the other hand, is crowded onto a peninsula. It has plenty of neighborhoods, small in size but still retaining their own unique character: Chinatown and North Beach (home of the Beat poets and City Lights Books), Noe Valley and the Richmond, Twin Peaks and Golden Gate Park. It has billed itself as "the city of poets." Luckily for us poetry thrives everywhere. Poets can speak from any place.

Doing a compilation dealing with just one town is difficult enough when you're wondering how to set the tone. My co-editor Bill Mohr and I had quite a time getting it right. He is predominantly a champion of Los Angeles-based poets, a former editor and publisher of one of the city's legendary literary journals/small presses, *Momentum*/Momentum Press, and author of a scholarly work on L.A. poetry. His eye guided me toward some of the people in L.A. I knew only tangentially, and whose time up north was unknown to me. I, on the other hand, with several decades of a frenetic life in my adopted town, added to the growing list of possibilities. We had to come up with people who had not only lived in both Northern and Southern California at one time or another, but who also worked as poets in both regions.

The two cities of *Cross-Strokes* share origins as Spanish towns built around Native American settlements: Mission Dolores in San Francisco, Mission San

Gabriel on L.A.'s outskirts. Intermittent, nagging reminders of a troubled past, these missions became the psychic centers around which the premier Gold Rush town of the north and the "Dream Factory" of light in the south would cluster: S.F. has its elegant Victorian architecture, L.A. its Deco edifices and anything else it can get its arms around. As one reads these poets who know both towns as poets truly in residence, we hope the reader will experience writing that speaks to the peculiar voice that is the West Coast.

This book is not at all meant to suggest that these poets constitute some kind of regional canon of the past seven decades. The "old man" of this gathering of poets, Kenneth Rexroth, who began in San Francisco, only to move south in his later years, always emphasized the independence of West Coast Poets. We agree. This book is a gathering of many voices — poets of the same terrain walking many roads. Bill Mohr and I celebrate the restlessness of West Coast poets. It is our hope that *Cross-Strokes* will serve as a guide to our wise, wild and wily coast, and that it will help to stir yet more poetic dialogue.

—*Neeli Cherkovski*

FRANCISCO X. ALARCÓN

Born in 1954 in Wilmington, California, a working-class town near the port area of Los Angeles, Alarcón graduated from California State University, Long Beach, and Stanford University He currently teaches at the University of California, Davis. He won the 2002 Fred Cody Lifetime Achievement Award from the Bay Area. His books include *Snake Poems: An Aztec Invocation* (1992), *Sonnets to Madness and Other Misfortunes* (2001), *From the Other Side of Night / Del otro lado de la noche: New and Selected Poems* (2002), and *Ce Uno One: Poems for the New Sun / Poemas para el Nuevo Sol* (2010).

Poor Poets

   to Miguel Ángel Flores

poets go astray
on the streets
like chicks fallen
from their nest

they bump into
light posts that
without warning
cross their path

courteous as ever
they ask empty
park benches
for permission to sit

nobody knows
not even they
why wings sprout
on their shoulders

maybe one day
they'll finally use
that key they carry
forever in their pocket

Pobres poetas

a Miguel Ángel Flores

por las calles
rondan poetas
como pajaritos
caídos del nido

dan con los postes
del alumbrado
que de pronto
les salen al paso

ceremoniosos
les piden permiso
a las bancas vacias
de los parques

nadie sabe ni ellos
mismos por qué
en los homros
les brotan alas

un día quizá usen
por fin esa llave
que desde siempre
traen en el bolsillo

From the Other Side of Night

what to say
about silence

the pages
left
unwritten

the books
in which
we are yet

to be
appear
exist

this life
condemned
to oblivion

here
nobody knows
nor will know

of the sea
we carry
within us

Del otro lado de la noche

qué decir
ante
el silencio

las páginas
que se quedan
sin escribir

los libros
en donde
todavia

ni somos
ni estamos
ni existimos

esta vida
condenada
al olvido

aquí
nadie sabe
ni sabrá

del mar
que llevamos
adentro

Sonnet X

Of Dark Love

"there are two ways in the world: to see
yourself one day in the mirror, or never see
your true self-image, to see yourself is to live,
not seeing yourself is death," you tell me

"look at me, I am more than my look,
more than a passing smile on a street,
more than piled horizons, the one who looks
at you is more than the one you look at"

"seeing myself in you, I discover who I am,
I want you to see yourself likewise in me:
looking at me, see yourself looking at you"

"look at me, for I see myself in you,
look at me, for you are my mirror,
look at me, I want to be yours"

Sonnet X

De Amor Oscuro

"dos caminos hay en el mundo: el verse
un dia en un espejo o el nunca llegar
a verse de veras, verse es vivir,
no verse, estar muerto," me aleccionas

"mírame, yo soy más que mi mirada,
más que una sonrisa en plena calle,
más que todos los horizontes juntos:
el que te mira es más que ése que miras"

"al verme en ti, descubro lo que soy,
así quiero que tu te veas en mí:
que al mírarme te mires mirándote"

"mirame que me estoy mirándo en ti,
mírame que tú eres espejo mio,
mírame que yo quiero ser el tuyo"

Mestizo

my name
is not
Francisco

there is
an Arab
within me

who prays
five times
each day

behind
my Roman
nose

there is
a Phonecian
smiling

my eyes
still see
Sevilla

but
my mouth
is Olmec

my dark
hands are
Toltec

my cheekbones
fierce

Chichimec

my feet
recognize
no border

no rule
no code
no lord

for this
wanderer's
heart

The X in My Name

the poor
signature of
my illiterate
and peasant self

giving away
all rights
in a deceptive
contract for life

BRUCE BOYD

Born in San Francisco in 1928, he was educated at UC Berkeley, where he met Jack Spicer. Boyd moved to Los Angeles in the early 1950s and was a founding member of Venice West. He moved back to San Francisco in 1958 and joined Robert Duncan's workshop. By the late spring of 1960, he returned to Los Angeles in search of remunerative work. His poems and prose appeared in *Evergreen Review, Yugen,* and *Floating Bear.* He was one of the poets featured in Donald Allen's *New American Poetry* (1960). Known as the Zen poet of Venice West, his whereabouts after 1969 remain unknown and open to conjecture.

Venice Recalled

on the salt water streets
that rose & then fell with the ocean
when the fish that were caught in the mud
underneath the wooden footbridge started in to stink,
soon there was always the incoming tide

                                                   there, we were
each his own man

       to speak, the play of sounds, pleasant or
       otherwise, but only open & discursive

                         differently, here, at the language
the oblique sense of a word to stamp one as "in"
                         whose dialect (not
dialectic) held
           "right or wrong"
invents a greater crime than just to force the song:
to force it back,
          & closets them wet & huddled together.
      they are fearful in their heads
      of being on the outside looking in
      — to the center of language:

but we who would live openly are its natural peripheries,
& take the unborn where the dead leave it
to grow, at our hand

"always to prefer the common," thus the noble
Heraclitus, in "this world, which is the same for all
      our language is although induction
      the topology of what we live:
      thus not its substitute but its enlargement.

                             there, with us
a new poem was something
                  the making, something
that asked to be shared at once: seldom a "result"
to praise or blame, & never this only, we mostly looked
behind it for the ways that came together,
between whom, intended, a clearing was being made

in which to discover what, having forgotten
is recovered
        in measure, apart from direction:
    as in accord with old codes,
    codices,
        a kind of love
    of least action in language, or
                taken as return
to the origin,
        a place of actual
welcome, always the nearest
stone path that is watered
            against the coming of guests
      is to say,
           cooler:
& the poem, what it means to say,
for the natural motion of its body, is the clearer
that remarks the wider movement of its actual thought.

NOW

so far)
a perfect sign

like rain on a slope too long a time dry
heard at night, now the turn comes,
                                    or felt
like former wars to set a bad peace back to rights,
with such delight, comes on
                        like a flood
of time to a place that knows what do once again
makes this to greet it

            or her
        the presence of whose grace I mean unfolds
        or seems to disenfold as if there were
        superior dimensions to the place, more light
        across the flood to follow to our lady of

        whom there is nothing to hold to

  : for the water subsides.   the afterflood of silt
sloughs off the land in flakes, & dries
& crumbles to a dust that daylight brushes
where the air expands across the field and half lays bare
this crust of bricks, that spread of bones, a heap of ash
    a perfect sign.

    "shall I cultivate these ruins?" to himself
    the learned gardener says.

& a city springs to the eye.

                    (XII.59)

This is what the Watchbird Sings, Who Perches in the Lovetree

Who has but dighted his tricks in a bed,
And never delighted in anything said,
He'll nibble dry leaves until he is dead.

For love is the kind of a tree whose fruit
Grows not on the branches, but at the root.

Who with his lover's real presence has talked,
And enacted his lover's least speakable thought,
He will find out what it is he has sought.

For love is the kind of a tree whose fruit
Grows not on the branches, but at the root.

Sanctuary

because the warm honey
      is never dissolved, by water,
but drifts on the river's stone bottom
like wads of raw silk,

under the surface the swimmers still look

    where sharp little stars
        bloom on the bone-tree
    & tender incredulous fish
        swim out of its watery eyes

& grow warmer; while gently the bone-tree
      is turned in its bed
    & sees how it gradually wakens

around it the water is still:
but the sheet glass surface is quietly shaken
& breaks into ripples, as gulls rise
into the room of the hungry children
to watch the tall water close over their heads.

NEELI CHERKOVSKI

Born in Santa Monica, California in 1945, Cherkovski grew up in San Bernardino and co-edited a magazine with Charles Bukowski, *Laugh Literary and Man the Hunting Guns*. After co-editing *Anthology of L.A. Poets* with Bukowski and Paul Vangelisti, Cherkovski moved to San Francisco where he worked on Beatitude magazine and wrote biographies and a critical account of West Coast writers, including *Ferlinghetti: A Biography*, *Whitman's Wild Children*, and *Bukowski: A Life*. Cherkovski's books of poems include *Animal* (1996), *Elegy for Bob Kaufman* (1996), *Leaning Against Time* (2005), *From the Canyon Outward* (2009) and *The Crow and I* (2015). He has poetry books in Spanish, German, and Italian and an English-language book published in Calcutta, India. He served as Writer-in-Residence, New College of California.

Nearing 69

these huge blue elephants
come into my room
I can hardly move
they have no respect for the furniture
or the paintings
they don't know that I'll be sixty nine
in three months
that it makes me nervous
they don't understand
the culture of youth
and the very human desire not to die
yet there is some indication
they have profound feeling
and mourn their dead
with a blast of the trumpet and a drum roll

I saw Jessica the other day
my old pal
now in her 40s
sitting in the café drinking white wine
like it was ice water
and Lawrence in his black beret
95 years old
taking healthy measured steps
into an imaginary plaza with a fountain
and a statue of Saint Francis

I seem to get confused now
parking in the space reserved
for a famous tech magnate
losing my place in *The Inferno*
and feeling sick for the miss-step

69 years
might as well be enough
when you consider

but I'll get used to it
and adjust
turn up the heat at home

eat less meat
stop craving young hot men
make myself useful as an elder
at a tribal council
of an island republic

69 chances
to make a break for it
69 tons of elephant
tromping in the hall
wrapping a trunk round a house plant
and eating it
along with the container

a baby elephant climbs onto the couch
and it collapses
a bull argues with his own image
in a mirror and butts it
the wall cracks

69 chances
to be a wise old man
like Zarathustra

and after 69
a deluge of sea water
over my chest
a sprinkle of stars

a hummingbird
in the air
by the front door

Hydra Waterfront

yes the water is perfect and
still, the Flying Dolphin leaves Piraeus
and skids on the Gulf
slowing only moments before
entering the harbor and gliding
to the waterfront, it's a rugged
land of rocks and whitewashed facades,

on Hydra the Venetian
palaces give supplication
to Helios, Jackie O visited
while I was there, and
Leonard Cohen
saw "a bird on a wire" which
landed in a song, there was
the British expatriate who
painted his way into an alcoholic
dream. . .

no, I haven't been there
for seven years, and you
were put into an old folks home
in Hayes Valley, assigned
to a room that looks out on a tree
and you liked to wander,
the attendants took care
to meet your needs

I'd come to see you
in advanced age,
eyes shining and
poems burning up
in a drawer, we had to
walk the waterfront
and feel the breeze

on Hydra once
I made love to a
young man from
Salonika, (Hal, he had

dark, hairy legs).
we spent five days in a room
by the port, the chubby
matron brought food and sweets
she would giggle, knowingly. . .

I honored your poems about every Hydra
sprinkled over many lands,
your shades of sensibility flowing
on the wharf, awake like a seabird
cawing at the action on the waterfront

you told me
about the donkey boy
who was hung
like a horse, was
he the wizened one
I saw gathering
memories on the
pier jutting into
the harbor?

I miss you more than I miss
you, I guess it is a feeling without
measure, you were the man
who showed me at least one way
out of solitude and back to the self

I picture you on Hydra in the 50s
sitting poised to write of the people
below your window, the
donkeys braying, crowds milling
across the water in the harbor
to those catacombs
below the poem

(for Harold Norse 1916-2009)

Funny Old House

we're in a funny
old house of three
rooms on three
floors, life is
a flood, life is a
sentence, life
is what you wring
from words, light
is where you go
to get out of
the darkness

in spite of us
the fumes rise
and convert us
to glowing orbs
of fire, we adore
the house, it is
really serious
once you caress
the walls and
shut a few windows

the first floor
is a kitchen with
propane stove, every
morning I brew
strong espresso
and read between
the lines, cross-wise,
my thoughts are
settling on a
garden in paradise

on the second floor
a bedroom, and
on the third floor
a more substantial
room with bath, we
go up and dawdle

all day unless
we're driving to Pisa

I am unable to focus, the
trouble is in getting
trapped, confused,
short-circuited, no end sight

is the end of this?
it is to the kitchen
I go, here in the
chill room a compact
refrigerator, it
buzzes, a cigar
burns, thunder
graces sky and
it rains, the door
is open, every
drop of rain has its own
awareness, happy
am I to put an
outspread palm
into the deluge

the propane
is precise, whatever
I cook sizzles or
boils with no problem,
the blue flames are
wise and meditative

to you who jot
a tune in a red notebook
with spiral binding I wish
to explain how fine
it is to sleep on the edge
of a bed in the Tuscan
hills, awake

what manner
of sadness? the bees
are splendid,
they serve tea

on the terrace,
a medieval tower
sticks its neck
in nearby Bagnone town

in a drawer your socks,
two pair, and two manuscripts
of writing, nicely
printed on 20 pound
white paper

blue facades trimmed
in white and white trimmed blue
is all I see walking the hills
of smoke
and ochre, nodding
to a woman who passes
every morning
as if from the earth
below her feet

(for Paul Vangelisti)

To the Poet at Twenty

you will not stay young
despite wildflowers
and the floating yellow lie
that covers us

you will grow grey hair
in a far distant winter
your eyes will see
waning light

you will be dazed
by loss of speed
in the haunting ballroom
where joy reigns

you will bury a mother
and throw dirt on her hair
and curse when your father
is covered by a flag

covenant remains
blue sun reigns
men will take pains
to tally their gains

black moon rises
with inhuman surprises
you will no stay long
The shadows will lengthen

you will test the night
with poems and vision
till the pen drops and
creation perishes
you will guard words
in the groves and on
the plain, the white stallion
bolting past the groove

you will find thunder
in the meadow, fire
on the sky, you will
tame the years

you will not stay young
your sound will deepen
I feel it in the bones
of December yet to come

MICHELLE T. CLINTON

Born in 1954, Michelle T. Clinton grew up in Los Angeles and began attending and eventually leading Beyond Baroque's poetry workshops in the early 1980s. West End Press published two collections of her poetry, *High Blood/Pressure* (1986) and *Good Sense & The Faithless* (1994). In addition to a spoken word project released by New Alliance records, *Blood as a Bright Color* (1993), Clinton's poems have appeared in several anthologies, including Bill Mohr's *Poetry Loves Poetry* (1985) and *Best American Poetry of the Year* (1994). She has also received a National Endowment for the Arts creative writing fellowship and co-edited an anthology of Los Angeles poets, *Invocation L.A.* She currently lives in the Bay Area, where she moved in the mid-1990s.

If somebody tries to give you something, let them. This applies to everything, especially cigarettes, sex & drugs.

Tell time to take a hike.

Laugh at everything you can.

Find people who are hanging & hang with them. Screen them with drugs: weed alla time, cocaine too hard on the pocket, beer'll make you fat & gin'll make you drunk a lot quicker. Slamming is hard on the nerves, green pills white pills & black ones from somebody's doctor play real well, & nobody crazy with good sense does acid.

Tell everybody everything. No masks, no mysteries & tell everybody you won't tell anybody, & tell anyway.

Figure out who is hanging with who. Go to people you don't hang with but know they hang with people you hang with, 'n say HOW'S DAH HANG?

Establish an in clique code word for those not hanging: ya got-cha basic square, ya gotcha pasty faced 'merican geek, bending over, goin' for the okey doke. Ya gotcha LA strangelo, & ain't nan' one of 'em know how to hang.

Open your home as a hang center. Keep tidbits in your freezer, Stock up on ultra-stress formula vitamin B complex. Do a lotta dishes. At least once a week, plan on giving over an evening to somebody's bad trip, somebody's peel, some trim together sculptor will do the break down & then you got to hang tough.

How to hang tough: Imagine yourself very cool, very sharp & altogether together. Remember it's fine to be crazy, it's like really okay to be crazy, like what the fuck else we gon' do, we got so much heart, so much insight, we livin' in a hellacious world, man, folks like us, if we wasn' crazy, we'd be dead or crazy ONE! Then tell your partner. Let him know who's boss. Confess something evil. Hold him. Tell him, again, his momma wasn't jiving, she does love you, man, she just didn't know how & it ain't nuthin wrong wit being crazy, & you ain't crazy no way. Be prepared to knock his ass out if he gets too wild.

Regarding sexual activity, consider filthy language and lingerie. Never sleep with anybody crazier than you. Unless you up for a wild ride. Keep your hands cupped over your heart. Do not fall in love.

The Emergence of Barren Women

In the fifties my momma got caught
in the back of a musty Pontiac
w/ her legs in a catholic koan
she wanted to do it & did
but got caught by a hard man
a missed period & me
soft bones & white spittle
me & my waste all over my momma's hands

As a child she dreamt of nursing
in white stockings w/ stiff cap
part of the colored elite rising in am. 1954
my mother the only colored speck
in st. teresa's school of nursing
first negress capped & pinned
after she finished nine months
she dropped out
when I dropped in her life

In the sixties I applied to Berkeley
& got on the pill
the threat of hard men
shrunk w/ the tiny secret
I swallowed each morning
in college I buried my catholic roots
& studied biology, feminist archeology
dissecting the remains of old women
the details of their waste, their patience
I moved fast the morning after
my blood was late, cheap & quick
needles & scraping, let me out
the trap, a clot of black & red cells
that wanted to shit all over me
& make my dreams useless as a mother
in the nuclear age:

my mother sits
my mother remembers
a nursing cap flattened
in the back of my father's car

More Gods Means Less Slavery

It is the one god that I hate
the one lord of all mighty & minute
stuff that makes me mad
his sticky clouds/   his science fiction
his book locked in on law & punishment
would shrink me down
the big daddy god wants my anger small
& my knees collapsed
the good sense of teachers & angels see nothing

Yo pops/   I said once
this is a day unlike any other day
when such & such & such happened
& blip tee blam went down
& I'm bumming
I'm in need of a clue
what's my next move/   mister man
kneel down/   he told me
suck up your gut
& act like a god damn man
& after you die
things will be better

But things being hard as they was
I figured his penis was the problem
so I shaped the mud of his body
into a giggling girl/   just like me
& followed the goddess followers
into the caves of female comfort
where the goddess of everything substitutes big daddy
where her angels sing lullabyes
that bounce off the surface of the world
& leave the oil in the ocean
the mess in the city
the cracks in bitter children
for the law of karma to cope w/
you create your own reality/   the goddess answers
keep your personal cubbyhole clean

The goddess of one is into denial

so she piss me off too
cause she ain't hip to psychic death
the soul dies easier than the body
the spirit can be murdered
the good sense of teachers nuns & angels see nothing
just say no way/ they tell me
big shit/   I answer
tell it to my cavities
sing it to the violence choked in my mouth
promise me on Halloween

So I let them both fall from the sky
gentle man & lady gods
I made them break apart
& every chip of holiness
is some kind of god I can use
cause when the one god broke
she/he expanded to include a bad
attitude & urban abuse

This is a poem about the triumph of shattered divinity
for example/   the god of orgasm sometimes makes an ugly face
the anti-god of time hangs out w/ the pseudo god of rent money
the first & last god I call on lives at the bottom of my gut
where bits of the smashed gods fell into me

If it weren't for the broken gods
I wouldn't have none.

TIM DONNELLY

Born in Los Angeles in 1963, Tim Donnelly grew up in Redondo Beach and was active in the poetry scene of 1980's Los Angeles; including the Beyond Baroque Poetry Workshop, hosting readings at Angel's Gate Cultural Center in San Pedro, and publishing poems frequently in *Shattersheet* and *The Moment*. A Berkeley poet since 1991, he helped found The Last Word reading series. His chapbooks are *Velcro Heart* (Shelf-Life Press, 1989), *A Season In Bed* (1998), and *I skip the long ones too* (2004). He provided drawings for francEyE's book *Grandma Stories* (Conflux Press, 2008).

the failure of nasturtiums

if only I had watered more
the Brinks guard would of been shot down anyway I might
have fucked up my back anyway
putting in wandering jew and creeping charlie
plants grow so fast their names are verbs

Nasturtiums everywhere
when will it rain anyway

my green thumb in this sandpit

we have plain old solid orange or streaked
all but the gorgeous poppy-red kind

the smell is nasty but in every one
is a tiny suckle of honey

I have seen them strangle out whole gardens
but not in september
or such deadly heat

The Spell of the Wild Wooly Mint

You have lived here too long she said
with jabbering walls with
doors that don't close
you have lived here too long to
be in suitcases and crates

You broke your good luck with both hands
she said these walls stare
can you even write here
do guests quarrel

A sphinx is a tomb to a dead
a smoker is a ladybug
the bed works without levers she
said she said
fifteen years

she said you will root again but not here

The Year It Rained All Year

I read *King Lear* to the
profoundly disabled. It took
a week. That's how they
knew I was mad.

Commercial radio featured
sad junkies and angry junkies.
Sponsored by auto insurance
and the diamond business.

The boy downstairs was 21.
He asked me repeatedly not to
stare at him and sigh.
Though he liked me close by.

My boss was a moulting spider.
I dated a speed freak who was perfect
in every other way.
The hallway smelled of pee.

The answer to any grievance was "El Nino."
The baby squalls and her tears
wash the air crystalline.
Sight and smell are sharpened.

The Night The Roof Caved In

The third crack was loudest
and followed by a boom
I was soaking in a deep warm tub
padded nervously toward the door when

the rain pool of swimming water
banged in my door deadbolt or no
I was met by an icy wave knee high
on its way to the kitchen

the bundled trudge in pouring rain
and soggy shoes to find a pay phone
the flashlight fireman barking pack fast
the whole place could collapse

the hotel room the lawsuit
the mold and the cheesy remodel
that took my claw foot tub
are all in the future

leave me naked and dazed
electricity still on
a winter creek run through my living room
when Jonathan next door commences to shout
a word beginning with the letter F
a word we all know

Former Gloryholes

What brine walls what slimed stalls
cower the hungry fingers and feet
of grown men and such legends as
show hard for BJ and
love to suck young cock

my cock felt old at fifteen
high on rollerskates and packed in cutoffs
gliding from public toilet to next
and what of those grown men with whom
I shared such brief illegal things

Liz and Monty

she cradles the head she thinks is dying
his human blood stains her blue taffeta
Roddy weeps silently
Rock blubbers
in a movie the car would burst into flame
not just hug the tree for solace

the first reporter arrives
his flash attachment huge as a satellite dish
she clenches her beautiful teeth and speaks the words
snap him like this and you never work again
take this picture and you will be
one sorry toad
he tells the others all there before the ambulance
this is a closed set

Elizabeth dropping her own hot tears
into the broken face of a friend

My Writing Helmet

The kid is twelve if that
Skinny, pale, scabby
This battle will be a joy to him
He is a man
See, he has been given a helmet
It will not protect him
He will not save his village
Or his family
His malnourished body will be slopped in two like nothing
He knows it
Smiles into the mirror for hours
The helmet is a useless thing
Strips of leather woven crisscross
Hanging down the back of his neck
It will not save his head
It will not save his neck
He grins as if he were given a helmet made of gold
He is a man

SHARON DOUBIAGO

Born and formally educated in Los Angeles, her self-education as a poet began after getting B.A. and M.A. degrees in English from CSU Los Angeles. She has primarily lived on the West Coast, and often made use of a succession of road-tested vans to extend the radius of her residencies in Port Townsend, Washington and Portland, Oregon. She currently lives in San Francisco. Her award-winning fiction includes *The Book of Seeing with One's Eyes* (1988). As well as her post-modern epic, *Hard Country* (1999), her collections of poetry include *Psyche Drives the Coast* (1990); *Body and Soul* (2000); and *Love on the Streets: Selected and New Poems* (2008).

The dress I was wearing when my brother was born, my bangs
growing out. My father
undressing me under the house
in Ramona my sister has reported
again and again, my white
Maidenform bra

I am trying to tell my sister
or someone downstairs
to save the rotting lemon
because it's organic. We can't remember
everything. We can't forget anything

the last hook, then snap of the band
with the half inch seams
I always had to make
both sides of the 34D
to fit my girl frame

The migraine up Clevenger Canyon,
there's a grainy black and white of this, I'm
16 in a white V-neck Orlon sweater holding up my heavy hair
having pulled over on that dangerous spot. Having
Vicki take the picture because otherwise
I'd never remember that I
had a headache.

Daddy and my brother were boys
but not different from me,
Mama and my sister. I thought of their things
and our things like clothes we put on. Male
and female, this is how I understood adjective.
I believed with the fervor of prayer we were the same. I still believe
we are the same.

Daddy in his bath shows me how he masturbates,
the word more forbidden than witnessing masturbation
and I don't remember through all the years ejaculation.
He lies in the tub, his big boned, white hairy body
in the bubble suds. His hairy toes turning on the hot water faucet

to reheat, that's how long we've been in here, his hairy fingers
around his purple thing

and what is a mistake? and what is remembering? what is
a sin, instinct, desire, what is
allowance of the self, what is
justice and what is love?

running away, disappearing into the fog
to Korea   to Europe ravaged
to the river bottom, my father
ravaged   Going back

to the house the first time after I told
my mother in the bathtub, last week of 6th grade. I remember
flying through the house, leaping off the porch
knowing the greatest relief I will ever know, Mama
will take care of it. But imagine
going back and Daddy coming home.
I remember her beautiful body in the bubble suds, I
don't remember going back to the house, I never
thought to try though she was never the same, I was never again
her child, I didn't know this until now. I always thought
my not remembering was good, this is how we forgive, this is love.
I so loved my mother and my father and my sister and my brother.

Last night I nightmared again
the murdered girl. What to do
with her body? I can't remember who she is
but I remember the Los Angeles River still free
though it had flooded before I was born
killing so many it had to be cemented.

I don't remember the Fathers' castrating me
stuffing my mangled, bloody genital into my mouth,
their faces can't be looked at.
I don't remember my gender, my father, my tribe, the fear
but I remember my mother is lost
so my heart rises to go to them
fleeing back down their many mansions
then unable to weep, to remember how we walked

the millenniums, each a galaxy of blood
a hundred billion ancestral faces looking up, if
you are found guilty, Daddy, will they execute you?

I remember my first song, "shu shu m' baby."
I remember going into that forbidden place, myself
that island rising up on the horizon.
I forget its name
but I remember when
it saved my life

Abalone

Abalone deep down there growing the waves
high up here flying, light and water
and earth and sky, abalone all along
growing thirty years now on this headland
writing, all this time growing my meat
my shell, my glisten, my suck.

The Pomo wore abalone to ward off sorrow.
Mid October, the divers keep surfacing - "Oh!
there's so many down there
you catch your limit in ten minutes"

keep pulling up abalone
roots of the waves, root of this sunset, red and silver
abalone the identical waveroot pattern. And the full Moon
coming up behind, all night sailing to the west
on the abalone clouds. O my glistening moon
will they pull you up too?

There was a pyramid of abalone shells
next to a pyramid of black bombs
on the black asphalt shortcut we took
Friday nights, coming and going
Terminal Island.

The bombs, black iron balls with fuses
were like the black marbles on our Chinese Checkers board.
The abalone shells were shiny silver moons, Egyptian
pyramid beside the Nile, as shiny
as the bombs were dull black.

TERMINAL ISLAND SINKING!
the headlines screamed
because of the removal of oil
for the war. Maybe,

the little girl in the back seat thought, if they removed
the pile of bombs Terminal Island won't sink. Maybe
if they quit removing the abalone from underneath
Terminal Island won't sink

Like Shasta's clouds now, she thinks, way north,
the same pattern, as above, so below
our flesh, our flyers, our glisten, our suck, O Love
our abalone moons once rooted, now wandering
from place to place
to ward off sorrow

PATRICK JAMES DUNAGAN

Born in Fountain Valley in 1974, he grew up in Orange County. He moved to San Francisco in 1998 to study Poetics at New College. In 2011 he published his first full-length book *"There Are People Who Think That Painters Shouldn't Talk": A GUSTONBOOK*. *Das Gedichtete* appeared in 2013, and *from Book of Kings* will be published later this year. In addition to a number of previous chapbooks, his poems, essays and reviews appear frequently in a number of publications. Dunagan lives in San Francisco and works at Gleeson Library at the University of San Francisco.

Lowell

Her head is smashed, gnarled in glass
I marry her because she writes
because she writes I hate her and tell her so.

The madness of the world pursues
buried in the poems and argument.
I win every time in everything I try

My heroes I assume in lesson upon lesson
(much of which I myself ignore, tapping out lines
time after time, listening in on sources.)

I have kindled the flame greatest of all.
She has told me so & so has she & she & she.
My daughter fills the glass, bringing it to me

song spills from her, she is of me & loves
only to live loving me. It is fair as is she.

Victrola Blues

> *I have seen the* David
> *And the* Mona Lisa, *too*
> *And I have heard Doc Watson*
> *play 'Columbus Stockade Blues.'*
> —Guy Clark

Mostly the black blues.
Let me tell you a little story.

His song "Doctor Jesus"
that would have been in 1928
the name that was just about to roll off my tongue
didn't have a bit of false pride in him.
He did it the way I did.

Dad and two of my brothers worked for an uncle
unbelievable, the things he could do

Merle and I, my boy, we loved the blues
when we got into the music together when
we got to know and love lots of the people
during the Depression.

All the fiddle tunes I could think of
trying to get her speech straightened out
I didn't know how I lost it.
I'm thankful that Dad wasn't a racist. My mother was, a little bit.

They treated us good.
Now you know how I think.
See with the feet and my hands and my ears.
I always sang in my own voice.

Reading Olson in Long Beach

Breeze ripple
in the absurd
palm-speak

such there is
no getting to
or from

out of mind
comes worry
as is said

gulls dive
'our body
is our soul'

for Lorca, & to Duncan McNaughton

Cognates

> *And who can square*
> *I want nothing at all*
> *With I want it all?*
>
> . . .
>
> *for that world when*
> *You didn't have to know*
> *What you know now*
> —William Corbett, The Whalen Poem

A familiar brawl
my hobby was to make a town
those furious summer evenings. . .
what you just don't say
I wouldn't bullshit you, wouldn't bother
confused love
an indoor garden party
teenage-published
party of ghosts meeting
two of them Bronte wrote of
the way into anything is retrospective
a very excessive novelette
left undone, directly lifted
capturing your mind
just getting started
eternal opening doors
already stepped beyond
different roads to familiar places
having a coke with you
one of summer's not-yet-here adventurous hours
life hits paydirt
signs masque
the hour family
drops its weight
sure asking favors
there's no denying
des drôles très solides
another set of trolls gone off

for Tracy

RICHARD GARCIA

Born in 1941 in San Francisco, Garcia published his first collection of poems in 1972. He moved to Los Angeles in the late 1980s and conducted workshops in art and poetry as Poet-in-Residence at the Children's Hospital Los Angeles for a dozen years. He has won many awards, including a Pushcart Prize and fellowships from the National Endowment for the Arts and the California Arts Council, as well as the Cohen Award from *Ploughshares*. His books of poetry include *The Flying Garcias* (1991), *Rancho Notorious* (1991), *The Persistence of Objects* (2006), and *The Other Odyssey* (2014). He currently lives on James Island, South Carolina, with his wife, the poet Katherine Williams.

Dreaming of Sheena

The sun wiped out the night like an eraser.
It was a morning fit for pancakes
but my lucidity found no outlet.
So I went back to my dreams, a groovy
dream of love, adventure, and terrorism
and Sheena of the Jungle in her underwear.

Sheena had skimpy, leopard-skin underwear.
Her thronged behind emptied my mind like an eraser.
Then, out of frustration, I became a terrorist
with explosives disguised as pancakes
and plastiques in my shoes that were groovy.
My mission: blow up the Eddie Bauer Outlet.

Or was it the Citadel or the Desert Hills Outlet?
I had ammunition stashed in my underwear.
It made me walk bowlegged but I felt groovy.
After a series of explosions I craved pancakes.
But they tasted like warmed-over pencil erasers.
I wanted to dream of love, not terrorism.

Or was dreaming of love a kind of terrorism?
But dreams of love were not the way out.
Let me find a woman with the scent of pancakes.
I searched for a phone number over and under.
Where could it be, I hope I didn't erase
her number from existence. Then—groovy

And cool, I found it and let me repeat, groovy!
I tried to focus and dial but I was in terror,
Isms of doubt crossed my heart like erasers
on a blackboard. Would I find an outlet
for my jungle passion sniffing her underwear?
Or was she really just ugly under her pancake

makeup? Could I be the one to butter her pancakes?
May her thighs snap shut on me! Here follow groovy
fantasies of Sheena underwater in her underwear,
Sheena with knife between teeth, Sheena fighting terrorism,
while I toss and turn, wishing for an outlet—
here follow galloping zebras striped black and white like erasers.

Would I wake to pancakes or love like terrorism?
Or might I wake yelling groovy or take me to the outlet!
May our underwear spin together or from my dreams erase her.

Naked City

She was the kind of gal who would look elegant
even if she was wearing nothing but handcuffs.
She had a way of leaning against a wall in an alley
that made you think she was wearing a gold lamé
evening gown, balancing an onyx cigarette holder
on her fingertips while a diamond bracelet
flashed from her wrist. When she sat on a bench
in the station house, doing her nails, humming
to herself, I said a silent prayer that she would not
raise her skirt to adjust her stockings. If she did
I'd have to think about baseball, which I despise,
or the locations of seemingly unrelated homicides
forming a crude calligraphy of her name on a map.
By now you've guessed that I was nothing to her,
an omniscient, voice-over narrator watching her sashay
in and out of trouble in a hundred different locations.
And what was that stupid tune she always hummed?
It was, "one-two-three the conga," the same one I found
myself humming after I brought her in for questioning
and got nowhere. It was "one-two-three the conga," stuck
in my head as I stood in the interrogation room, alone,
rubbing lipstick from her Styrofoam cup against my lips.
So I thought I could latch on to the small waist of happiness
and follow it anywhere, but pursuing happiness
is like pursuing a murderer—it has its depressing moments.

Their Words

He was fond of saying
"machete" at the most
inopportune moments;
for instance, while
they took a bath together
and he sat behind her,
his legs wrapped
around her hips,
soaping her back
with oatmeal soap
he'd whisper in her
ear, "machete."

She called him
"My Little Escarpment."
He didn't know what
she meant by that.
Was it something muscular
and slimy, like escargot?
Or did she think he
was her balustrade,
someone she could lean from
and wave to a passing crowd,
someone she could leap over,
or climb up on with a rose
clenched between her teeth?

If he was in a really good mood
and she asked him to work
in the garden, maybe
trim the rose bushes
he'd say, "Get the machete."
He liked the sound of *g*
slashing through the *e*'s
and knocking against the *r*'s.
"Let's have a daughter," he'd say,
"and name her Machete."
He imagined an
eleven-year-old girl
boys were afraid of.

Machete, willowly blonde
with a pony tail, sweet,
sensitive Machete, but stern
with an eleven-year-old's
sense of justice, and a tiny,
crescent-shaped
fencing scar on her cheek.

Once he spent several nights
crying out in his sleep
in what seemed to be an ancient
Middle Eastern language,
perhaps Babylonian.
It was during this episode
that he sat suddenly upright,
in a cold sweat, clutched his chest
and whispered, "Nunishmu, poison
arrows of darkness have got me!"

Her highest exclamation was not
words at all but a low,
teeth-clenched, sputtering growl.
That's when he knew
she was truly happy.
He'd feel as if
he were floating,
carried along under stars
in the narrowing circumference
of a vast whirlpool.

S.A GRIFFIN

He was raised primarily in and around Richmond, California. He migrated to Los Angeles in 1978 with a scholarship to attend the Los Angeles Civic Light Opera Workshop and has been a working professional since. Carma Bums founding member, he has been publishing and editing on his Rose of Sharon imprint since 1988, and was the co-editor of *The Outlaw Bible of American Poetry* (1999) and *(Sic) Vice & Verse* (1992-1999). In 2010 toured the U.S. with Elsie The Poetry Bomb in an effort to inspire civil disagreements. In 2014 Griffin published his most recent collection *Dreams Gone Mad With Hope.*

There is a River

there is a cheerful ignorance
a chance meeting &
luck like gold that cannot be
mined or
stolen

a common atom

a dance

& stars that trick the
water with their
certain
magic

do not wash your wars in it
take your holy rituals to the
precious fountains built by your
agencies of fear

press your
wine from the fallout
& drink your
bitter victory

for yes

there is a river
a giving river that will
sing you safely

a river of
light

final
fast
& free
where you can
disrobe
& leave your casual sadness

walking sideways at the
shore

meet me there
whoever you are
& we will agree to
swim it
together

I Choose Not To Believe In War Holy Or Not

if I were Christ I would be a drink of water
if I were Buddha I would gladly kill myself
      in the garden of your eyes forever
if I were Mohammed Mecca would be the journey in your touch
if I were a Jew the holy land would be the covenant of my blood
      singing hosanna in your veins
if I were an atheist I would call your every footfall god leaving
      footprints in the moment

Genius

a dangerous word
full of guilt and promise
often misunderstood
much less if ever
defined or fulfilled

there is genius in ignorance
more than one could ever design
into the hysterical awe and wonder of the greatest bomb yet to be
or the mayhem of microscopic conclusion
franchised by the architects of fear

genius wears black
believes in the rubric crucible of death after death
rides the feral roller coaster of depression
arms raised high
& negotiates the aether of
falling dreams one foot in front of the other
with verse

calls history liar
& weeps openly over the most casual cliché
breathes art
bleeds light
befriends trees
& everything yet to know

wears the untrained hair of a nervous garden
& is learning to play Gershwin's Rhapsody
on Picasso's blue guitar

   when walking into a room
   most experience eggs, water, salt, sugar & flour

   others taste cake

Weapons of Mass Destruction

she was studying Dante's *Inferno*
for her senior lit class

we sat side by side in 3rd period art

"Why are liars in a lower level of hell
than the murderers?"

impressed & curious
that she would
defer to me
on something I hadn't read
I gave it a beat
then surprised myself,
"The truth is,
that the murderer probably only
kills one person.
The liar can potentially
kill millions, like Hitler."

satisfied she had her answer
we shifted subjects
& continued on with our
drawing

she was more beautiful
than I could have known at the time

Vietnam was waiting for me
rents were cheap & inflation
was just appearing upon the
landscape of our Yankee lexicon

if we only knew

JACK HIRSCHMAN

Born in New York City, in 1933, Hirschman was educated at City College of New York and Indiana University. After receiving a Ph.D., he took a position teaching at the University of California, Los Angeles, from which he was fired for his political activism. He moved to San Francisco in 1973, where he continued to work as a prolific poet, translator, and radical social activist. In 2006-2008 he served as Poet Laureate of San Francisco. His books include *A Correspondence of Americans* (1960), *Black Alephs* (1966), *Lyripol* (1976), *Front Lines: Selected Poems* (2002), *The Arcanes* (2006), and *All That's Left* (2008).

Balaban

I ran down the street and into the house smelled
of oregano and shook Mickey Monaco, said
C'mon, Balaban's got a breadloaf
Climbing over old Gruber's fence, he thinks
the mad dogs is doves

But Mickey grew up in the bed till he was too old
and besides, Balaban was crazy, he sucked
his tongue and got left back twice

So I ran to Joey Bellino's house but his mother's
black stocking said Joey was out early shoe
shining, And besides a, that Balaban he's a
crazy a kid, he suck a the tongue and Joey says
he got lefback twice

So I banged on Bitsy Beller's window yelled he was
near the top, the mad dogs waiting down below
he thinks is doves

But when Bitsy stood up he turned into a stiff
cue stick. And didn't want nothing to do
with nobody cracked upstairs.
And Dickie Miller became a semipro. And Howie Fish
a doctor. So I ran down the street full of hope

by myself because I was on fire. But I got there
too late for Balaban. Two of them had a stretch
of skin between their teeth fighting over it,

and the foam of the mouths and Balaban's blood
spattered in such a way, the most the greatest
looked me straight in the eye, made me
sit in the gutter and cry,

and when I got up vow to be
Balaban from that day on.

The Burning of Los Angeles

Smelled her before the eyes saw her
    going east from the sea on Sunset
got a whiff of her through the smog valved exhausts
      nagging motor grind of the winding road
She was lining them up for miles at the pass
    of the freeway under me

Supple up there licking the tops of the trees
chewing the hair offa them
    A deer came down a canyon with
      a piece of her and done
    A palomino came down his mane was her and died
at the edge of the gutter
        with jacarandas died with cries
of muskrat leaping from trees
thumps of rabbits on stone
                Screeching and whine of
sirens of engines ambulance spotlight
out of the awe of my eye

Broke into a cold run diagonally across my legs
    in front of me up a canyon drive
She smelled deeper the closer I came natural
    red white and black
The higher I ran Man against wall upon roof
    with piddling garden hose
A colt in agony but I never looked back
And she'd bitten the wrists and calves of a poodle
    and three other bitches who ran from the heat
could see her slithering a thigh against a rooftop
More and more trees saw her blowing black
    and blue through morning smoke a hole of sky

They were coming down away from her nails her
        teeth cadillacs jaguars a chauffer
            in profile what wildness of Laugh-eye
And a moose with the body of a man came running down
And a trophy she kissed one side of the sun gone tar
        black bellies of pillows with goosefeathers
and jewels stuffed Picasso
ran right passed
            Renoir

Crazy it was dada with czars and jews both gritting
        with bitten cigar-ends angry cuts
A couple of kids pointing Wow she's nekked
The cops thick around
            the spouting engines
clubbing her hard nails banging her ankle cops
with boys at the corner of their mouths wanted her
hip to hip cops with
            Handmedownhose
cops nada cops nuns in pain gasmasks to keep from smell
her rich armpits the mole in the middle I hide in
dry brush watch them spit
at her bite at her paw

And how she fumes and fangs back booms windily from
        inside a house spits billions of windowglass shells
Rears up like wall water falls upward by the santana whips
            the fuzz on their cheeks with cycloon gives
            them wilderness eye throws back
her hair blasts their faces with blush says
                C'mon you can do bettern that, says
                Why din't ytell me at the edge, says
        This is no place for kids, bends

And scatters them so many pins with one roll and uproar
        of a fireball and I light I light up
            right then and there
                we're alone no sound but the sirens
        and spittle high back in her throat
She's smelling me out she's not saying No she's not
        saying Yesbut she's not saying anything but
            lean I can see her
            step out of brush

                    window lean up against Wall
light up the corner of her smile a
      Click of sheer mesh of
              of stocking of sullen
                    backless heels clacking
Time it was
            Time on high street with the great again
grandmother of every whore gig sweet you
And she laughs a whole stable of
flaming bluebloods spill foaming whinnying out
veining down the canyon a carpet of
Meat for my leap
      And I leap

The Whole Shot

In Memory of Gregory Corso

Most, given the death we've all been given
before we die, die.
Greg didn't, Greg wouldn't, Greg ain't.
He burned his being burned and being burned up
right in front of you,
up front,
in your face, he was a fighting little neighborhood,
city-wide.
I never saw him sing, he never sang, copper,
O but he sang.
And guzzled and fixed and trashed and mashed.
Consumed. He was consumed by consuming,
competition's fool
from Maldoror through every lowdown kind of
kinahoor clear down to his own stretch marks
in Dannemora.
I went to see him in the hospital once
when his head, 3 times its size, some blood
he'd dissed in the drunk-tank had kicked in.
Which was after he'd once right-crossed me
for no good reason, like my best friend the
Calabrese kid in my neighborhood in The Bronx.
Which was before a bull-dyke once decked him
For dissing lesbians, and for being monstrously cute,
humiliating in public to women and men alike,
a self-styled "rotten fuck" who never cleaned up,
a nice guy who said, "No more nice guy,"
all brag and loudmouth blow,
fame up his ass
"I'm Gregory Corso"
like at a horseshow,
provoking, stirring shit,
yelling, "Hey, Ginzy!" up to Shig's place on Grant St.
when Allen was visiting, for some dough.
Or: "Hey, Jackie, where's Neeli? He took
Max for a walk?"
In this bar or that, running with this or that mug,
that chick or this,
toking in an alley or back in the john,

or cross-legged serious in the Caffe Trieste
reading the *Chronicle* or *The Times*
mixing it up with a mouth in a gallop
like Billy Hallop
with twinkle and charm out of hell,
he was one of a kind
of a devil character,
so you might never have known
he could precision an image
to its finest fain.
turn a phrase and make it sit in
with a combo of sounds
that unearthed a flagrant poesy
from ancient undergrounds,
write from a spring
without himself in it
and make the running diamonds
"the whole ball game"
or "the stiff arm of Cuba"
more than just sport,
"the whole shot"
in the senses that toppled
lying news reports,
taking one's breath away
and leaving a real gape suddenly
sprouting daisies in your empty spaces,
the way it is when you're met
by a pair of eyes on the street
above a mouth that might say anything,
above a body that might do anything,
yet those eyes in a slow, smiling
recognition rise and wink:
"Hey you, human bean, you Poet,
You synecdochal yokel of all,
nothing's concealed,
nothing's hid.
Cross my heart and hope to live."
The Kid is dead.
Long Live the Kid!

LENORE KANDEL

Born in New York City in 1932, Kandel grew up in Los Angeles. Her first collections of poems was published in 1959, after which she moved to San Francisco. In 2012, North Atlantic Books published *Collected Poems of Lenore Kandel*, which included *The Love Book* (1966) and *Word Alchemy* (1967). *The Love Book* had been the subject of an obscenity prosecution in San Francisco in the mid-1960s; the initial conviction was overturned on appeal. Kandel died in 2009.

Emerald Poem

there reaches a point without words
    safe   a point deep within the emerald
    seabright washes over eyes and tongue

frozen the stonebirds fly soft among my fingers
their tiny beaks tapping snowflakes from my thumb
        the color of emeralds
the solid becomes the liquid and I the greenbreather
I am at home among the nebulae
      in the heart of the emerald
    safe   a point without words
one is one and I the green breather
      I the gill singer
oh the liquid green flowers that the small birds carry!
    they fade to lavender
      on my tongue
    they fade to lavender on my eyes
oh the stars that devour me in the heart of the emerald
    safe   in the flowers of the emerald
    safe   at the point without words

Invocation for Mitreya

to invoke the divinity in man with the mutual gift of love
with love as animate and bright as death
the alchemical transfiguration of two separate entities
into one efflorescent deity made manifest in radiant human flesh
our bodies whirling through cosmos, the kiss of heartbeats
the subtle cognizance of hand for hand, and tongue for tongue
the warm moist fabric of the body opening into start-shot rose
    flowers
the dewy cock effulgent as it burst the star
sweet cunt-mouth of world serpent Ouroboros girding the
    universe
as it takes its own eternal cock, and cock and cunt united
    join the circle
moving through realms of flesh made fantasy and fantasy made
    flesh
love as a force that melts the skin so that our bodies join
one cell at a time
until there is nothing left but the radiant universe
the meteors of light flaming through wordless skies
until there is nothing left but the smell of love
but the taste of love, but the fact of love
until love lies dreaming in the crotch of god. . . .

Peyote Walk

1

VISION: that the barriers of time are arbitrary; that nothing is still

we, the giants of the river and universe, commencing the act of
love, enclosing our bodies in each other's wilderness, vast hands
caressing pinnacles of meat, tracing our titan thighs

       one month we touch extremities
          next year a kiss

the giant prick engorged began its downward stroke at years
beginning into years end giant cunt (a) (slow) (sea) (clam)
hips and rotundities earth-moving from month to month and
promises of spring

    orgasmic infinity
    one (!) second long

       EARTHQUAKE!
   FLOOD! FLOOD! FLOOD!

    huge pelvises shuddering
    while words burn

2

VISION: that the barriers of form are arbitrary; nothing is still
now now   now
         moving
tangled my fingers tangle in
     sticky life threads
         moving
between my fingers
a geode, granite walled crystal universe
I see both sides at once
how easy   why didn't I before

I AM
part of the flow

    the lamp the fig and me
    we the redwoods
    us the walls and winds
       body mine?

    you?
MOTION

beingness   my fingers t-
      angle

the only light our vital glow our radiance
turning to you your face becomes a skull
    MY SKULL!

protean the form encloses space and time
    moving

NOWNOWNOWNOWNOWNOWNOWNOW
    NOWNOWNOWNOW

    3

VISION: that yes
    (we)   is   (god)

from *First They Slaughtered the Angels*

I

First they slaughtered the angels
tying their thin white legs with wired cords
and
opening their silk throats with icy knives
They died fluttering their wings like chickens
and their immortal blood wet the burning ground

we watched from the underground
from the gravestones, the crypts
chewing our bony fingers
and
shivering in our piss-stained winding sheets
The seraphs and the cherubim are gone
they have eaten them and cracked their bones for marrow
they have wiped their asses on angel feathers
and now they walk the rubbled streets with
eyes like fire pits

STEPHEN KESSLER

Born in Los Angeles in 1947, Kessler attended UCLA, where Jack Hirschman was one of his professors, before receiving his B.A. in literature at Bard College and his M.A. at UC Santa Cruz. From 1979-1985 he was the editor of the international journal *Alcatraz*, which featured such Los Angeles writers as Wanda Coleman, Charles Bukowski, Kate Braverman, Dennis Cooper, and many others. During that period, he was also a regular contributor to Papa Bach Bookstore's magazine, *Bachy*, where Leland Hickman served as editor. His thirty books include, most recently, *Where Was I?* (2015), *Need I Say More?* (2015), and his translation of Luis Cernuda's *Forbidden Pleasures: New Selected Poems* (2015). He lives in Santa Cruz.

Vallejo Remembers

Do you still make that little buzzing sound
between your teeth when your lover is coming?
You were the only woman I ever knew
who did that
and it was immensely sexy
20 years ago?
or whenever it was we were given our time together
and here comes the sound of the cable-car cable
heard from your bed
as it hummed and clanked under Mason Street
and the tall glass of water you always placed on the nightstand
and your fluffy white terrycloth robe and the down comforter
and your mandolin or was it a balalaika?
and when I lay behind you cradling your little breasts
you'd grind your butt so deliciously into my belly
those nights on Russian Hill
just up from Keystone Korner and the police station
on a street named after a Peruvian poet
still reach me sometimes when I'm in the neighborhood
on the border between the smells of the Chinese fish markets
and the erotic garlicky aromas of the Italian restaurants
red wine running through our brains and tongues
there was something radiant about those hours
so what if you made a habit of being late
it's so much later now
what matters is what endures of our connection
brief as it was
a certain indelible residue
of tenderness

Synchronicity

The obscure poet in the grungy overcoat
hitchhiking one gray day up Highway 1
was someone I knew because in 1966
he'd come and read to our class at UCLA:
Introduction to Poetry, Jack Hirschman presiding,
chainsmoking Pall Malls, staring out the window into the smog,
and raving Blake and Rilke, Whitman, the Greek Anthology, Dr. Seuss,
Genesis, "apocalyptic consciousness," and something he called
synchronicity.

So Kirby Doyle was the guest one day;
he read his "Ode to John Garfield"
unforgettably but I forgot
until I saw him hitching on the coast,
pulled over, picked him up, and greeted him
by telling him who he was:
"You're Kirby Doyle."

The bridge of his disbelief was blown—
it got him going—
all the way into the city he spewed prophecy:
         "If things keep going the way they are
Evel Knievel will drive the Earth right through the Sun!"
         "I don't believe that God will be able to prevent
the transparency of genetic flesh."
         "Never make your muse your mistress."

It's longer ago tonight from that afternoon
than that day was from his Haines Hall reading—
yet here they are,
up-to-the-minute as Huckleberry Finn,
old as Sappho's bones
nostalgic with desire—
and there you are,
cruising L.A. in my car,
playing your postpunk tapes,
filling your tank on my credit,
and drinking margaritas with other men.

Chaos Theory

Hitler thought the stars were made of ice.
Sometimes astronauts drop their screwdrivers,
which orbit Earth until puncturing spacecraft.
SWAT teams do not administer CAT scans.
Ogden Nash and Dr. Seuss
never appeared on the same stage.
What in the sky rhymes with time?
Answer: a herd of clouds.
Showering outdoors in early winter
one feels invigorated, temperate, elect,
whatever calamities are occurring elsewhere—
proof this world is probably the best.
Do the math.
It all adds up. Saul Bellow said so.
One is born under a deadline with no outline.
You open the blank blue book for the final and let fly.
What can be told alone in elliptic loops
ordinary prose obscures. Logic is like
a backhoe violating nature with a straight line
in which to lay pipe for plumbing.
Freely one fails to detail
a full accounting of experience.
The mere thought of it turns you vertiginous.
The words come back stamped insufficient.
What string stroked by which bow
resonates in Sinatra when some snotnosed
mafioso is stomped in a parking lot
in darkest Vegas
and no policeman or comedian
appears to stanch nor even hand
a hanky to snivel into?
This is the whole cloth and nothing but,
a form of crime and confession at the same time,
only without the law—
except for those blinding lights by the roadside,
the same scary cruiser that comes to the rescue
after you've failed to arrive,
your career a skid.
Whose voice is that? Oh, just a late poet
on the radio, taped ages ago, now resurrected

and echoing spookily. There goes
the old vain pain of losing the youthful looks.
And look at this: the large dog
suddenly takes a bite of the child's face.
Everything that falls erodes the road down,
its ruts arrested for a spell by blue shale
over which we roll
slowly
moving out toward mail.
You want to know so what.
I can't say except to sob,
muffled by retort before I start, doubtful
whatever I report
will make the cut. Mushroom poachers
skulk through the woods toting plastic bags.
Supermarket clerks decode *The New York Times*,
sounding those little beeps, 7 cents tax.
One might as well surf naked
carrying a torch at midnight under a full moon
and be seen only by lonesome werewolves
or startled cosmonauts dropping their violins,
which is that strange sound you may hear circling,
something like the great discoverers
crashing lost into blind lands
to which they gave wrong names in ignorance.
Know what I mean?
You drive like that
and they take your license away,
leaving only a noise of noxious revving
to *wha-wha* in some garage.
Remove gravity and men drift on wind.
Warning to mice: you may ignite if you bite wire.
Above traffic, trees can be heard trembling.
Cricket-gossip, coughing frogs, doomed moths rattling lampshades
and hungry skunks on front porches rummaging through kindling
make wild music amid tall thickets
of randomly blooming volunteer arugula.
It doesn't take a rocket scientist.

LEWIS MACADAMS

Lewis MacAdams was born in West Texas in 1944. He graduated from Princeton and also attended S.U.NY. Buffalo. He lived in Bolinas, California from 1970-1980 and was the director of the Poetry Center at San Francisco State University from 1975-1978. He moved to Los Angeles in 1980 and edited *Wet* magazine for two and a half years. He was the founder of Friends of the Los Angeles River. He has published over a dozen books of poetry, including *The Poetry Room* (1970), *Africa and the Marriage of Walt Whitman and Marilyn Monroe* (1982), *The River: Books One, Two and Three* (2007), and *Dear Oxygen: New and Selected Poems* (2011), edited by Kevin Opstedal.

The Soccer Field

As night falls, the people start heading north,
coming down the canyons, clutching paper sacks
full of belongings, as the electronic
warriors of the north tense.

Behind their brush mustaches and computer consoles,
on their horses and in their ghetto birds, gripping the wheels
of their pick-up trucks,
they already understand the utter futility of their mission.

Chopys told me he swam across
the Rio Grande 19 times
before he finally made it.

It's like holding back the future with a string.
The hunger that is driving these people
is more powerful than an electronic battlefield.

Hunger thrills us with its power.
What we want, what we have to have,
what we cannot be denied.

> *Buying a taco at a taco stand —*
> *a slab of plywood laid across*
> *a pair of sawhorses —*
> *beneath a bare light bulb*
> *at the end of a cord stretching back*
> *into a Tijuana apartment; then stepping through*
> *a hole in the fence and heading north..*

> *—Nov. 8, 1989*
> *As the Berlin Wall crumbles*

Supper in America

"It's great to stir something really thin
      that starts to thicken
            because you've put
                 a little flour in it."

Top Banana

Phoebe slips a curved blue spoon into
the soft mouth of Ocean, then
retrieves it from his lips. The baby
frowns, he grins! He can dig it!

Ohio Blue Tip

I don't understand the phrase "occasionally the dancer,"
so I ask Barbara Dilley what do you do "occasionally"?
She is quiet for a few minutes, picks up the book of
matches and says "It's like occasionally I dance."
Do you dance consciously? "A feeling. It's a feeling
of acceptability..." She shows me the box of matches.
Ohio Blue Tip. They are, as far as I know, the best
wooden matches for striking the place that is hot.
Dan Smith does about one art work every year
and it is hot. The pulse, she said,
is hot. The place of the work, she said
is receptively hot. Torque, she said, is the torque of the town —
JEE_ZUS! Admit impediment. Let the confusion
go through. Define its form. It's a decision that I
don't want to stop. The innocence of a child, you know?
How do you accept awkwardness in an adult?
In yourself. So many people come up and say oh,
you were just fantastic tonight.
And I was awkward as hell.
One man's awkwardness
is another's grace,
is intimate.
What do you mean "intimate"?
Is meshing of skins,
is shard knowledge, is somehow touched
without being felt, by another's man's grace.
It's a calling, somehow.
I remember someone saying "The blues is calling,"
and since then I have been conducted by the music
to a place where the human body carries the music
through the places and times.
These are the Time motifs for the dancer in space.
My body — This time — Is the space.
Consider *your* beat, or pulse.
I have only scratched the surface
containing the mystery that lies beneath
the words "occasionally the dancer."

It's a state of mind that you have occasionally.
What do you have the rest of the time?

The mind is a muscle, Yvonne Rainer said
R-A-I-N-E-R. The indians say there are two kinds of dancing
One you do before gods.
The other you do before breakfast.
You hitch up your pants,
stagger into the kitchen, and pull out
some eggs and bacon, heat up last night's potatoes,
pour some milk and orange juice into porcelain cups
and say yummy yummy yummy I've got love in my tummy.
There's a beautiful line in a J.D. Salinger short story
where a little boy pours his sister a glass of milk. He says
"It's like pouring god into god, if you know what I mean."
The dance you do before god is the dance you do before men.
Burning, when my consciousness is asked.
It goes on with you all the time, too.
I mean, with you and me.

Will Barbara Dilley,
occasionally the dancer,
inhabit *Ohio Blue Tip*,
an incognito temple
at Paula Cooper's Gallery,
while a baby
does it in a dream
to a star?
Barbara, how do you live some place?
How do you inhabit?
I bring my suitcase, my perfume and my toothbrush,
my unused sleeping bag and my moonstones
to Agate Beach. I bring my love-cross eyes
to my critical facility
and pray for union
and just rewards.
What else do you pray for?
Do you really pray?
Yes, I guess I do.
I don't really pray classically, I guess,
But I do it consciously. Dicky Landry said
that Duke Ellington said
that his music was just great prayers.
Just prayers, without hope of deliverance.
I hope that while I am alive I will know something about home.

Solitude Conundrum

The cigarette smoke curls
around me in the one
bright light above my head.
If it is true
what the Buddhists say,
self-disgust
is the first step toward enlightenment,
then I am on the road again.

Dear Lord of language,
of gesture and of moves,
lead me on.

PHOEBE MACADAMS

Born in 1947 and raised in New York City, Phoebe MacAdams moved to Bolinas, California in 1970 after living briefly in San Francisco. She lived in Bolinas on and off until moving to Ojai in 1982. In 1986, she moved to Los Angeles where she taught English and Creative Writing at Roosevelt High School until her retirement in 2011. She was a founding member of the Los Angeles Poetry Festival and of Cahuenga Press. Her books of poetry include: *Sunday* (1983), *Ordinary Snake Dance* (1994), *Livelihood* (2003), *and Touching Stone* (2012).

Happy Birthday Bolinas

for Joanne Kyger

Good morning, Joanne. This country is two hundred years old.
One green car. One white car. One convertible.
The heart is a muscle, the heart is a door.

Dream 1: I am in a concentration camp. I am on the beach. The water is black.
I am standing by the wire fence. I am talking to someone outside the wire. We
are standing face to face talking. There is no difference between life outside and
life inside except the wire. I am in the apartment of the commandant. I undress
in front of an empty bed. I get in bed and make love to the air.

Dream 2: There is a car machine, stripped down. There is a driver somewhere.
A voice says, "Now you have to make another one." The second car will be
identical to the first. A death's head.

Dream 3: I go out of my house to the pre-shamanistic exercises. We do splits
standing on our hands in preparation for the shaman movie. I am awkward.
The woman teaching is a shaman. She has silver discs on the tops of her hands
and on her palms.

I mean, our conversations make a difference. It has to do with words.

Every morning I came to the table and said, "All I want out of life is to live in
the grace of the Holy Spirit." The tone was honest and the words fell about in
the length.

The song is resilient. The song is a muscle.

Birds fly over, grass moves in the breeze. Rational Mind, you are so stupid, here
in the morning, in the gentle aching where the door is open the view is clear.

The Sounds of the City

I drink vanilla decaf, grateful
for the quiet and also for the chimes next door,
the rumbling city sounds, dog barking down the block.
You can rest in the sounds of the city —
something's going on, not intruding,
but you relax knowing it's always out there
and although you do not have to,
you can anytime just walk out the door
and see about those chimes
check out that dog
or walk to Skylight Books
to find out exactly what time the poet is going to read on April 14,
then go next door to Fred 62 and
have a green salad with balsamic vinaigrette and a plate of pasta
    pomodoro

or not. You can also stay exactly where you are
and watch the daylight fade on the fragrant geraniums of
    Mariposa Street,
wonder where those people in the plane overhead are going
    anyway
or contemplate the spring evening more generally, have another sip of coffee,
settle in. It's Passover, you remember, and the Angel of Death has spared us
    again:

something is moving, not death, but a breath passes over us,
and also stays, sitting with us, saying yes,
that is what I meant,
that is it, exactly.

The Memory of Light

For years, watching people on the beach
reminded me of letting go of yesterday
or of the fire on Black Mountain
which filled the Ojai Valley with smoke.
Firefighters came from India
and the blaze burned through Sisar Canyon
north to Jameson Lake.

I remember when the days unraveled
in tangles of children and chocolate,
fierce daisies and bodhisattvas,
when only the protection of
poetry stopped me at street corners
as our cars reeled out of control.
I could see poetry like
the line at the side of the road,
driving over Mt. Tamalpais in a dense fog
with the driver's side door open.

Memories come like a chair
thrown through a picture window;
like babies and madness,
they come through North Africa
on wooden slippers of adventure.

Orion moves slowly from East to West.
We chart it, find Polaris and Lyra
as we lie on a blanket in Frasier Park
and watch the light from a million years ago,
Andromeda tilting over us in the night sky.

11/20/03

NATHANIEL MACKEY

Nathaniel Mackey was born in Miami, Florida, in 1947, and grew up, from age four, in California. He received a B.A. from Princeton University in 1969 and a Ph.D. from Stanford University in 1975. He is the author of six books of poetry: *Eroding Witness* (University of Illinois Press, 1985), *School of Udhra* (City Lights Books, 1993), *Whatsaid Serif* (City Lights Books, 1998), *Splay Anthem* (New Directions, 2006), *Nod House* (New Directions, 2011), and *Blue Fasa* (New Directions, 2015); and an ongoing prose work, *From a Broken Bottle Traces of Perfume Still Emanate*, of which four volumes have been published. He is also the author of two books of criticism and editor of the literary magazine *Hambone*, whose twenty-first issue appeared in 2015, and coeditor, with Art Lange, of the anthology *Moment's Notice: Jazz in Poetry and Prose* (Coffee House Press, 1993). His awards and honors include election to the Board of Chancellors of the Academy of American Poets in 2001, the National Book Award in poetry for *Splay Anthem* in 2006, a Guggenheim Fellowship in 2010, the Ruth Lilly Poetry Prize from the Poetry Foundation in 2014, and Yale's Bollingen Prize for American Poetry in 2015. He lives in Durham, North Carolina, and teaches at Duke University, where he is the Reynolds Price Professor of English. He has previously taught at the University of Wisconsin, Madison (1974-1976), the University of Southern California (1976-1979), and the University of California, Santa Cruz (1979-2010).

Asked his name, he said,
"Stra, short for Stranger."
Sang it. Semisaid, semisung.
"Stronjer?" I asked, semisang,
half in jest. "Stronger,"
he
whatsaid back. Knotted
highness, loquat highness,
rope turned inward, tugged.
Told he'd someday ascend,
he ascended, weather known as
Whatsaid Rung... Climb was
all anyone was, he went
on,
want rode our limbs like
soul, he insisted, Nut's
unremitting lift...
Pocketed
rock's millenarian pillow...
Low
throne we lay seated on,
acceded to of late, song of
setting out rescinded, *to
the bone* was what measure
there was. *To the bone* meant
birdlike, hollow. Emptiness
kept us
afloat. What we read said
there'd been a shipwreck. We
survived it, adrift at sea...
An awkward spin it all got,
odd
aggregate. Occupied. Some
said possessed... Buoyed
by lack, we floated boatlike,
birdlike, bones emptied out
inside.
We whose bodies, we read, would be
sounded, *We lay on our backs'*

low-toned insinuance tapped,
   siphoned into what of what aroused
      us arrested us,   tested us
                      more
    than we could bear...
                  Loquat
   highness's goat-headed look's
   unlikely lure... Lore made of
less-than, more than he'd admit,
               muse
   made of wished-it-so... Ubiquitous
    whiff had hold of our noses,
    nostrils flared wide as the
  sky. Gibbering yes, that must have
  been how it was, what there
             was
at all a bit of glimpsed inwardness,
  buffeted cloth, bones in black
          light
    underneath... *To the bone* meant
             to the
   limit, at a loss even so,   eyes,
   ears, nostrils, mouths   holes in
our heads a stray breeze made flutes
            of,
   rungs what before had been water,
   bamboo atop Abakwa drum... An acerbic
    wine dried my tongue, my top lip
    quivered. "Perdido...," I sang,
             offkey.
So to lament beforehand what would
  happen... Rope what would before have
               been
breath

•

Whatsaid sip they lit Eleusis
with it seemed. Barley mold
　　made them wince... Heartrending
sky, held breath held high
　　　　　　　　　　　as a cloud,
　　Hoof-to-the-Head knocked hard,
　　no bolt from on high but their
　　lips' convergence came close,
　　　　　　　　　　　　　Maria
ruing the movement of ships...
　　The sunken ship they at times
took it they were on　　　no sooner
　　　　　　　　　　　　sank
　　than sailed again. Failed or
soon-to-fail form, sisyphean
　　　　　　　　　　　rock,
　　rough, andoumboulouous roll.
　　　　　　　　　　　　Serpent
　　wave, serpent wing, hoisted rag
　　snapped at by wind. Flag she
　　saw he lay bound up in, insisting
　　　they'd meet again. Lag anthem
　　suffused every corner, music
　　　　　　　　　　　　more
　　the he she saw,　　we the escaping
　　they, calling out names no where
　　　　　　　　　　　　　we'd
　　arrive would answer to, nowhere the
　　　　　　　　　　　　　　louder
we'd shout

Dark wintry room they lay shivering
in...
    Late would-be beach they lay
under the sun on...
      Sarod strings dispatching the fog
from Lone Coast, fallaway shore
    they lay washed up on...
                    Their
    lank bodies' proffered sancta
                  begun to
    be let go, Steal-Away Ridge
    loomed larger than life. Extended
    or extinguished it,   no one
could say which,   the soon-to-be
                    saints
      arrayed in rows at cliff's edge, our
       motley band uncomfortably among
      them. A school of sorrow seeking
                sorrow's
    emolient, albeit seeking may've meant
     something more, older than seeking, re-
    mote coming-to, barely known, of a piece,
                    beginning

    they broke taking
hold

WILLIAM J. MARGOLIS

Born in 1927 in Chicago, Margolis served in the U.S. navy after graduating from high school, but only briefly used the G.I. bill to attend college. After a period of wandering in the early 1950s, he settled in San Francisco and edited *The Miscellaneous Man* (1954-1959) as well as co-edited early issues of *Beatitude* with Bob Kaufman. After being severely injured in a fall from a second-floor window in San Francisco in 1960, he moved to Southern California, and became friends with Stuart Perkoff and others in the Venice West and Temple of Man scenes. In Los Angeles, he edited one final issue of *The Miscellaneous Man* as well as one issue of *Mendicant*. His collections of poetry include *The Little Love of Our Yearning* and *The Anteroom of Hell*. He lived in Seal Beach for many years and died in 1998.

Entropa

We waited for the sleep
of others images,
lulling our woes.

She was filled with chaos,
as was I,
all our malice gone.

It hurt, she said.
and she said she wasn't
used to it at all, yet.

I agreed, even though a man,
ostensibly stronger (a stranger)
& I said, "Sometimes I forget

at night, forget the disorder
in my life & limbs, forget the darkness
of this night . . . at night I forget . . .

& I open my eyes
& remember . . .
& cry . . . ."

And she was crying too,
in the presence & malice
of that chaos, that loss . . .

But the sleep came, of images
& hopes . . . & gave form
to our sleepwalking eyes,

Lulled us with light,
the light touch
of a dream . . .

Monterey, October

we sat on a box, she & I,
at the end of the wharf,
& we sat close to keep warm,
& I put my arm around her
for the first time . . .

the lights on the wharf
& on the boats
& all over the bay
shivered in the cold light
on two seals just before us,
& we watched as they
dove & came up & snorted
& dove & came up again . . .

farther off, somewhere beyond the boats,
beyond their maze of masts,
beyond the cold weird lights
we could hear the loud squeals and barks
of a herd of seals, invisible,
& we sat there in the warming dark
of our touching hands, speculating
as to whether or not
the seals were making love . . .

The Tide

the tide comes in
like a lover's arm
tossed in tired sleep

and we do not know
the splitting ocean
buoys us, wears us down
like chastened stone . . .

under a shattering moon
we are washed, driven
up a frightened shore,
cast upon the oblivious sand
like lovers, driven to purity . . .

from the sea we came,
and we lie upon the shore
limp and glistening, shaken
by our sudden birth to air,

and with the sun we waken,
laugh, and run through the fingers
of the drying sand, alive

DAVID MELTZER

David Meltzer was born in Rochester, N.Y. in 1937. His parents moved the family to Los Angeles in 1951, and he attended Los Angeles College and UCLA. between 1955 and 1957, during which time he made forays into Venice West. He moved to San Francisco and became the youngest contributor to Donald Allen's anthology, *New American Poetry* (1960). His books include *The Dark Continent* (1967), *Yesod* (1969), *Arrows: Selected Poetry 1957-1992* (1994), *No Eyes: Lester Young* (2000), and *David's Copy* (2005). He also edited anthologies and collections of interviews with poets as well made many audio recordings. He taught at the New College of California for many years.

The Veil

so sheer between what's right
and will be wronged
let's say the Taiwanese couple
on stage tonight in their launderette
washing and drying clothing
watched by two teenagers
in a non-descript Duster
windows fogged over with
potsmoke, fear and talk
with one gun between them
and an idea to rob
not for money
but to knife that veil
between them
and the good life

In the hole he counted heartbeats
but got scared they'd stop
listened to broken pipes
under the shit-hole in the floor
finally read the Bible they give you
but his religion wasn't in a book
unless it's the telephone book
so he stayed alive counting
letters, commas, periods

The veil

existed before he was born
and between his arising
shadowed the world he moved through
reaching for dim forms he thought
brought light

It was perfect
and we're all good at our jobs
but someone imperfect
bumped into the gun
looking somewhere else
and all hell broke loose
but it was only because
we're good at our jobs that
everyone got away clean

The veil

between what's called heart
and the real evil

TV cameras and goons
monitor constant rebellion
whispers, life —
sustaining schemes

Everyone listens
for their turn
like Shaharazad
keep the axe away another day

Listening and telling
learning how
but never the same again
inside or outside
utterly clear
about the real evil
and what is called heart

The scar

of that moment
without time
clocked rage
knife thrown at
Lilith
lands
half into my left
pinky
half
onto the table
time begins in sudden pain
wound's mouth pours
reassuring blood
onto wood

The veil

the moment when nothing is left
no control
a blank
time gone
her kitchen knife
in your hand
in her heart
and a new life begins
in the old fear
running out the door
buried with blood
everything too clear
the lights
no where to go

How cold

outside and inside this iron
I nightly write against
on paper she once wore as bride
down burning stairs
for my love

The piercing

Sunday late noon
a needle through his thumb
straight through it
the thread almost laughing
moving in and around
what would no longer be
a fingerprint on file
sworls of skinweb pierced
torn open just a bit
and blood managed out like a sap
he sucked
knowing full well there was no snake
except in his head
asleep, mutating

ALEJANDRO MURGUÍA

Alejandro Murguía was born in Los Angeles in 1949, was taken to Mexico at the age of six, and returned with his family to Los Angeles at age sixteen. He attended Los Angeles City College and moved to San Francisco in the early 1970s. He became the first director of the Mission Cultural Center in 1976. A short story writer as well as a poet, his collections of stories include *Southern Front* (1990), which grew out of his activism in support of the Sandinista movement in Nicaragua, and *This War Called Love* (2002). In addition to a memoir, *The Medicine of Memory: A Mexica Clan in California,* He has published several collections of poetry, most recently *Stray Poems* (2014) He was appointed the sixth poet laureate of San Francisco in 2012.

Mujer, mujer

You say you're going to go
when twilight plays beneath my eyes
that when you leave
I'll hear your song again.
And you're right my love
and you're right at that...

I have seen you sitting
at grey dusk
weaving the threads of life
playing the minstrel
singing songs with no lyrics.
Your images have floated back to me
blurred and sharp
muddy and clear
white and brown...
                    at times a lover
indeed at times a whore
and in the wake of the afternoon a witch.
But you're young and don't know
what lies beyond these bedroom walls
and have never seen your people hungry
or felt your spirit broken
nor gazed from my windows
towards the black alleys
cold and cutting thru the asphalt
like meandering rives

                    running thru our lives
                    running thru our lives...
I remember the guitar
that strummed across the summer nights
the haunting melody to passion
in the days when you were queen
and I the jester.
                    Those were the times my love
in the days when I was young
following you behind mirrors
of false society
and down lanes of white amerika

everything you showed me was ugly
you touched my hand
and your fingers were cold

and I felt lost
and I felt lonely...

So now you stand with your bags packed
                    ready to leave the streets that gave you birth
and go wandering amongst hands
                    that have no pity
                    and words that tell no truths.
But one day...one day
mujer, mujer
you're going to come back
wearing their clothes
speaking their words, doing their things
and I'm going to lead you
down the alleys where we fought
and the streets where we played
and I'll show you the rooms where we made love...
you're going to see your people
whom you abandoned and deserted
y mujer
vas a llorar.
Mujer, mujer
vas a llorar.

Caracas Is Not Paris

Caracas is nothing like Paris you said. As if any place could be like Caracas. Cesar Vallejo had also lived in Paris and had died in that massive city of alleys and rancid puddles of human piss stinking up the subways. Vallejo had written about his Paris in *Poemas Humanos,* my own copy worn at the spine. And now here was the book again, resting on your lap, as you paused to smoke a cigarette, with the ennui of a chanteuse. The café in the Latin Quarter was filled with students, most of them exiles from places like Chile and Argentina and every other country of Latin America. Yours was Venezuela, but more than that it was Caracas. Like a caress in the humid Caribbean night scented with plumerias and menaced with billy clubs—that was your Caracas you said.

Later that night the band kept playing a vallenato "Gavilan Pollero" and wine and smoke and friends and nostalgia for somewhere else, which is the purpose of Paris, the essence of that city. To feel exiled, to live exiled. Until you read Vallejo's poem I did not understand the word. It was the dead of night, the candles out, you were on the bed, staring at the ceiling, when you recited "Piedra Negra Sobre una Piedra Blanca."

In Barcelona years later I would recall you for no reason when I heard the stories of the executions on Montjuic during the Spanish Civil War. At the end of that night in the club, as the band put away their instruments you fell into my arms sweet as a mango in the mercado. With the others watching I circled your waist while you smiled and it seemed to me a unique occurrence, Haley's comet prophesizing the fall of Napoleon.

Vallejo died during the Spanish Civil War you said in the Louvre while you showed me the dead statues when all I really wanted was to look at you. As if Paris existed as a backdrop to your walk, sashaying across the boulevards, a red scarf around your neck, your hair in braids. You were more than anyone could ask for in one life time. Your voice, your words still echo in my own exile, without country or flag.

I did not believe you— believe what you said when you said you believed in the way you believed. But you meant what you said and I hope you never forgive me for doubting you.

You talked of streets that swallowed children, where rivers of sewage ran between the rows of houses and in those black waters mosquitoes thrived like flowers. And in the barrios children died daily for lack of aspirin or clean water. And right next to the most wretched hovels on earth rise magnificent palaces of marble and exotic woods where lords peer over the chaos like gods from the heaven. A city of skyscrapers and nightmares.

Guajira where your grandmother came from. Walked twenty-two days with four kids and no money to reach Caracas. But you were raised in the rich part of town and now in Paris on a scholarship you wanted to meet someone different, someone exotic and how more exotic can you get than a Chicano in Paris, you said.

You would recite Vallejo's poem in the dirty rain of Paris as we sloshed our way through the Latin Quarter, one thousand years of urine staining the pavements, and the poster of Rimbaud upon which I too left my yellow trail at the feet of the queer poet. Cars rumbling somewhere, a bus honking, children shouting in the apartments, our shoes squeaking on the wet cobblestones, and above it all your voice. Your haunting voice—*Me moriré en París con aguacero.*

My copy of *Poemas Humanos* so read and re-read and yet not a place mark on it, not a dog-eared page, not one fold or wrinkle on it, but worn down at the spine from the many times it has been cracked open in Paris, Mexico City, Los Angeles, San Francisco, the pages yellowed, frail and brittle like our lives.

I remember your body on the narrow bed, the areolas of your breasts, your hair spread on the pillow, the sense of being alive—young, in Paris, sipping coffee at a sidewalk café. But you would have none of it, the harsh cigarette and your black coffee. Your tiny grotto sparse as a nun's cell.

In a field beyond the soccer stadium dogs scavenged human bones and human fingers. You had worked with the forensic students exhuming the bodies. Whose bodies I asked. All our bodies you said. Our bodies so fragile like the dawn breaking over the llano and the parrots fleeing the first rumblings of the big cats, the jaguars, the panthers, their yawns like cannons roar, echoes of ten thousand years ago, still alive. The song "Gavilán Pollero"—thirty years later I can still hear it—*Gavilán, gavilán, gavilán. Te llevaste mi pollera gavilán.*

Caracas grew old and withered because you were not there.

Paris was beautiful not because it was Paris but because you were there. And Paris without you would have been dead as all the dead soldiers of World War I, when people in the City of Light died of disease and famine and those that survived ate rats. And every animal in the zoo was eaten, including the ostrich, the red foxes, the white rhinoceros, all the monkeys, and the lions. The citizens of Paris spared nothing to stay alive. It was scorched earth all the way. The Army sweeping the llanos of campesinos, like the Parisians had swept clean the zoo.

You couldn't stay there in Venezuela, even though you and your country had the same name. You couldn't stay here either—a bourgie med student on the Champs Élysée where your less than ice pale skin made you stand out, and children on the street pointed to your black hair in braids.

"*Me moriré en París—y no me corro*"—Walter dead now floating like Shelly in the waters of Venice—L.A. that is—poet wanderer to the end, his copy of *Poemas Humanos* on my desk and your memory with it.

Those nights in Paris spent in your studio, somewhere I don't remember, but do remember you, the shape of your waist, the mint taste of your mouth, your dream of Caracas like blue phantoms on the wall. You dreamt of children without hunger or tapeworms, of water without deadly amoebas, a world simple and clean for the children.

And you knew your dream was as wild and desperate as Vallejo's dream of a free Spain in 1938 when the fascists crossed the Río Ebro and everyone knew all was lost.

The Orinoco runs through your life like a savage rain carving the land. One afternoon in the city where I live the Spanish language television said you were killed in a shoot-out. You had an alias but I recognized your description. I turned off the television, the rest didn't matter. It wasn't in Paris where you died; it wasn't even on a Thursday.

It was Caracas—so many years ago, so many. But I still remember how you read that night in your grotto by candlelight, by cigarette smoke, your voice filled with blood and sweat and crimes and murders and redemption of a whole continent, and finally the words you knew so well—because they were Vallejo's, but also because they were yours too. And now Vallejo's poems linked forever to you and to Paris. *Poemas Humanos* yours forever in life and death and Caracas. Everywhere lovers dream of a better world you will be there, you and Vallejo.

—*Tal vez un jueves, como es hoy de otoño.*

San Francisco, Califas
June 2011

ERIK NOONAN

Born in Los Angeles in 1974, Noonan grew up in Sherman Oaks. He attended Hampshire College, Utrecht University, and New College of California. Under the imprint Snag Press he published a magazine called *Weigh Station*, along with collectible chapbooks and a series of zines. The author of numerous articles on art, film, literature and music, his books of poetry include *Stances* (2012) and *Haiku d'Etat* (2013). Noonan is currently writing a book about the poet Paul Blackburn. He lives in San Francisco with his family.

Glam Squad

the early-nineties death mask started to peel

we stitched on some chevrons, teal & puce
without anesthetic
our work looked great
then we blundered into a fable
fully furnished with market categories
got a taste of who the boys are into
alluring objects crowded the flickering gloom
so you "dug" them, big deal
what distracts us at our washstand
is the perfect distress "a careful
negligence" as Ben puts it
bus driver has not learned use of brake pedal
synth pink dusk

Lovescape

uneven shade like a thin wash on fine paper
props vaultless sky over plateglass the color of purgatory
an Angeleno palette remains autumnal, frostbitten
some seasons even St Ives squints Florentine
azure neon proves life still gets high someplace
no fixed relation here no long cold line of sun
no repose nothing lonely there never is
just Baxter Northup in the aureate air
I can't make out from my motel balcony
what studio copywriters life deals with otherwise
morale turns septic not citric new suit or old
john stall where youth and beauty pass away
celestial bodies breed showmantic bluster in fools why
we each felt the rest were in a dream the whole time

Fairest child of flowing time

though no such time existed nor did the place
I suppose in old parlor pagan England
where Cowper notes Prior's "ease" meaning poise
tillage as livelihood or gardening as pastime
stays daily real like labor's and leisure's face
who each imposed decorum on the other from next door
yet also conjures up all sorts of lives
that might severally cultivate tact as grace
which spares little room for human passion
but go ask about commitments you'll find
a fictious metaphor like Venus flakes out
on hers no less than Christ has his from the start
hence this strange urgency of fluent numbers
when we measure out our hymns to the spring

HAROLD NORSE

Harold Norse was born in New York City in 1916 and educated at Brooklyn College and New York University. He lived in Paris at the notorious Beat Hotel in the late 1950s and early 1960s, after which he moved to North Africa. In 1968, he relocated to California, first living in Venice, California and then moving to San Francisco in 1972. He died in 2009. His first book, *The Undersea Mountain*, appeared in 1953, and was followed by *The Dancing Beasts* (1962), *Karma Circuit* (1973), *Hotel Nirvana* (1974), *Carnivorous Saint: Gay Poems 1941–1976* (1977), and *In the Hub of the Fiery Force: Collected Poems of Harold Norse 1934-2003* (2003). In 2014 Talisman Books published *I Am Going to Fly Through Glass: Selected Poems of Harold Norse*, edited by Todd Swindell. Texts for the poems included in this book are from this volume, which features an introduction by Neeli Cherkovski.

Island of Giglio

we sailed into the harbor
all the church bells rang
the main street on the crescent shore
hung iridescent silks from windows
stucco housefronts gleamed
rose, pistachio, peach
and a procession sang
behind a surpliced priest
carrying a burnished Christ
when I set foot on shore
a youth emerged from the crowd
barefoot and oliveskinned
and we climbed up rocky slopes
til dusk fell and close to the moon
at the mouth of a cave we made love
as the sea broke wild beneath the cliff
skeletons of fish, boats
on the beach, granite
boulders, juniper trees
and the town with winding
alleys; old men suck pipes
as the full moon leaps
like a flying fish &
shrinks up the sky; we
merge on the rocks
where waves run
up & down

Rome, 17.vi.54

At the Café Trieste

The music of ancient Greece
and Rome did not come down to us
but this morning
I read Virgil's *Eclogues*
struck by the prophecy
of a new era:
"A great cycle of centuries
begins. Justice returns to earth,
the Golden Age returns," he wrote
30 years before the end
of his millennium, describing
the birth of the infant god, come down
from heaven. Jesus was 19
when Virgil died at 89.
Will the Golden Age ever come?
Same faces throw up each generation,
same races, emotions, struggles!
all those centuries, those countries!
languages, songs, discontents!
They return here in San Francisco
as I sit in the Cafe Trieste.
O recitative of years!
O *Paradiso*! sings the jukebox
as Virgil and Verdi combine
in this life to show
this is the only Golden Age
there'll ever be

Classic Frieze in a Garage

I was walking thru the city past umber embassies
    & pine-lined palaces
        palmtrees beside balconies
    the heat something
    you could touch

    past three kids with cunning
      delinquent face
begging cigarettes
    from American sailors

−I thought of Nerval *Rends-moi le Pausilippe*
    et la mer d"italie
while living on the hill Posillipo
    above a gangster's dance floor

        on the bay of Naples
                in a stone cottage
    over tufa caves where the sea
    crashed in winter   sweet Gerard
        one hundred years
    have made the desolation greater

the tower is really down & the sun blackened
beyond despair loudspeakers advertise
       from boats on the bay
drowning out finches & roaring sea-caves
    all in the hands of racketeers

I have passed my time dreaming thru ancient ruins
walking thru crowded alleys of laundry
    outside tenements with gourds in windows
& crumbling masonry of wars

when suddenly I saw among the greasy rags
    & wheels & axles of a garage
      the carved nude figures
      of a classic frieze
      above dismantled parts of cars!

garage swallows sarcophagus!
   mechanic calmly spraying
     paint on a fender
observed in turn by lapith & centaur!

the myth of the Mediterranean
    was in that garage
    where the brown wiry youths
    saw nothing unusual
      at their work
among dead heroes & gods

but I saw Hermes in the rainbow
   of the dark oil on the floor
    reflected there
    & the wild hair of the sybil
    as her words bubbled
mad & drowned
    beneath the motor's roar

Naples, 1958

KEVIN OPSTEDAL

Born in Venice, CA in 1956, he attended St. Mark's Grammer School in Venice, and St. Monica's High School in Santa Monica, and haunted the poetry stacks at Papa Bach's in West L.A. and the Either/Or Bookstore in Hermosa Beach. In 1976 he moved north to Half Moon Bay. Among his numerous books of poetry is most recently *California Redemption Value* (2011), and his new and selected poems, *Pacific Standard Time*, will be published 2016. Opstedal is the editor/publisher of Blue Press Books and is currently living in Santa Cruz.

Fading like a feather of excess acetylene

Drinking cough syrup with John Keats
in a dream
on the bluff at Pacific Palisades

I can see the little warning lights of madness
flickering in his heavily medicated
bloodshot eyes

& leaning into the cold wind
strains of surf guitar
slicing in off Santa Monica Bay

and so Baja, Punta Baja,
Pipeline, The Wedge, High Tide (by the Lively Ones)
lend a dark twang to the
clear almost perfect blue

as if this wasn't the End of Days . . .

O angel of the abyss

Milarepa filter cigarette

Tracks

                                        of filtered light
shafting through stained-glass camouflage
            drains the sunset
broken up with headlines
                        of what's lost & won.
                            I can't call
love
        for example turning
her wrists a kind of silver
                    against the glassy surf the
shimmer of that reflected—

When the wind picks up in the eucalyptus
            like a vacuum cleaner surfacing in the South Pacific
I get the bends

Playa de los Muertos

The inside of my skull felt as though it had been scraped with a table spoon.
I spoke to leaves that skittered past on the pavement. Time sped up then
slowed down to an agonizing crawl. If it was true that the mind & the body
were one then I was fucked. Once on a beach just north of Malibu I left my
body for a while I think. I watched walls of sheet glass stand up like vertical
swimming pools then crash soundlessly in on themselves. It was all very
quiet. The girl I was with said later that she thought I had died. I thought so
too but didn't want to say so. She had blue eyes that seemed almost silver.
There were broken things in her head. I guess that was something we had in
common.

Chinese Algebra

That you render the silver
thread of dawn
with unerring fingers strumming the lead edge

tapping a dark vein
& all the broken promises
we've had to plow through to get here

Knowing the fatal intimacy of a bent
fender rattles in the stoke of too many perfect
days strung out along the shore I thought
leaves a little something for the soul to feed upon but

swept up in that rush & outside of time
limits the scope of your tender indifference
& drags the sky away from the horizon
at the winged insistence of gulls

for example

to qualify your absence
even before you turn to go

Placed against the edge of your breath
w/scant fearing
                          gust nor gale force would subsume
& by this random steps & redefines
the way it falls . . .

              I should know better having reconvened

                        to sift horoscopes & bend the tide
                 lifting that consolation to accentuate
                              your stark confines & rippling pavement

I guess tinseled waves
                    or folding sheets of bluegreen
glass when seen from outside
            section the predetermined measure
                                of your pulse

as you reach the end of something you
never even knew began

Stuart Z. Perkoff was born in St. Louis in 1930, and dropped out of college in his freshman year to move to New York City. He moved to the West Coast in the early 1950s, married, and eventually settled in Venice. Along with Bruce Boyd, he was a founding member of Venice West and was the first proprietor of the Venice West Expresso Café. After serving several years in prison in the late 1960s for a drug offense, he moved north to Mill Valley and Larkspur for two years and resumed writing poetry with renewed fervor. He returned to Venice in mid-1973 and died of cancer in 1974. His books include *The Suicide Room* (1956), as well as a pair of books from Red Hill Press, *Alphabet* (1973) and *Love Is the Silence* (1975). *Voices of the Lady: Collected Poems* was published by the National Poetry Foundation in 1998.

Untitled

human blood is its own
cartography. man knows
the distances, alone
& huge within the flow
islands of purity
great caves of death embraced
by flesh, the map of history
on which all pain is traced.

the flesh is muscle-clamped to bone
bone on bone on bone, to structure
a bone cartoon, which strives to make
a balanced tension, prone to rupture
on feet unlikely for their function
their stolen shape twisted, the horse
whose hooves they were, extinct. he found
them too clumsy to pace the course.

"my meat eats me" says roethke. i eat it.
eventually everything is food.
all life is dying, death is life completed.
in the same flesh, living is death renewed.
a flow of generation & return
more deathless than man's lust
to be divine. yet rage & terror burn
man's blood bubbling the dust.
flesh is not taught to trust
enormous rhythms. nothing it can learn
from what it holds within itself denies
the foredoom of its own decay. flesh dies.

Variation on a Letter to Jonathan Williams

Yr mention of Zukofsky
brings to mind
others,
poets little read. Of his
I remember parts of "A" scattered in magazines,
a poem
in an old *Poetry Chicago* called
"Mantis"
& a few others.

That is not a life. A life's
work.

       Others have left
           (with me
                even less

A man named
Herman Spector
in & around *Dynamo* in its day

Sol Funaroff
          who chanted to gatherings
all that pain & sympathy

Harold Rosenberg
turned philosopher

      Arensberg, collector
of paintings

        Is he dead?
Are all these men dead?

        Of those alive, which one still
writes at the poem?

Yes, Zukofsky
is still swinging "A"
thru the world

but the others /
a mystery.

What do they record,
I wonder, from wherever they are?
What do they record, of their lives
& visions of loneliness?
                        What do they say
of us?

ii

the word.
its value.   & weight.

Man, are we in, then, a dream
by inmates?
                think, man! call
into yr head, this picture,
the poet
            (by which I mean myself, or you, yrself, man,
standing hobbled to his wall
& striking out in his crippled fashion
at the world that he feels, at him, tearing

& these men! All these men
standing as he stands, there, & they too,
striking striking

                        see us as standing
without them,
think it man! Hobbled & halfblind
with them there!

                        & what of them? I cannot even
                        begin to imagine the extent of their
                        aloneness

A Suggestion to My Fellow Citizens

imagine revolutions have occurred! yes! why not?
& revelations! more! love! more! communal joy!
forget the rules, the rulers, the restrictions
which limit every action, every flight
of grace & wing, create
instantly yr ideal
city! its market places stocked
with fulfilled desires wrapped in images
unknown, but known to be
lovely as yr selves. extend yr arms & dreams
& see how interlaced a web
is structured by yr separate human needs.

The Swing

up in san francisco, dig, he sd /
                              speaking then
of language
                    (a concern that
            occupies our needs
                    currently

newness
in the word
the structure, like they say
or
in the swing of a line
a sound

using, he sd, the word in sentences
as brake up the flow of thinking /
        up in san francisco, dig, you dig
to shape the swing
to the tongue of a different eye
& I, thinking of the word,
                    like,
as used to destroy a reality
within a described scene

                    this changed line
of language, swung out
as we do it

                    lines of thought
unknown
on the other side of the Grass

what might it not do, to verse, to thinking

an attempt, at any rate,
now carried on

Untitled

black burnt hills
touch snow at their backs

trees cry
& lay their whiplike arms along the ground

stark bushes
bleed red flowers onto cold wet earth

birds of shadow
        flying
        flying
on a hill of green
        as tho
long after us

        everything renewed
        & clean

Letter to Jack Hirschman

jack, let's talk
abt
the streets. OK? where
it's all
happening, right?

what do we want from them? not
more blood, more graduate courses
in human capabilities. dachau
was the streets. how many more
such roads
must we travel?

let's insist on vision
i will accept nothing less than miracles
all men are unhappy
camus said
& everyone dies. a street
all share

perhaps it is a matter
of language
                 the sage says: man
is the language of
god. what creature or monster
forms our world
in its mouth?

where we walk
we know the dangers. if
the choice is between the streets
& literature
there is no choice

maybe we shd be talking
abt "joy." Is that what you mean
by "streets" jack?

KENNETH REXROTH

Poet, translator, essayist, and cultural gadfly, Kenneth Rexroth still simmers in memory as one of the prime instigators of the West Coast poetry renaissance after World War II. Rexroth was born in 1905 in South Bend, Indiana; orphaned in 1919, he spent his adolescence living with his aunt in Chicago. After a considerable amount of travel in the U.S., Rexroth moved to San Francisco with his first wife in 1927. He lived there until 1968, when he moved to Santa Barbara to teach at the UC campus. He died in 1982. His collections of poetry include *The Phoenix and the Tortoise* (1944), *The Signature of All Things* (1950), *The Dragon and the Unicorn* (1952), *The Collected Shorter Poems of Kenneth Rexroth* (1967), *Collected Longer Poems of Kenneth Rexroth* (1968), and *Flower Wreath Hill: Later Poems* (1991), all from New Directions.

from *On Flower Wreath Hill*

I
An aging pilgrim on a
Darkening path walks through the
Fallen and falling leaves, through
A forest grown over the
Hilltop tumulus of a
Long dead princess, as the
Moonlight grows and the daylight
Fades and the Western Hills turn
Dim in the distance and the
Lights come on, pale green
In the streets of the hazy city.

II
Who was this princess under
This mound overgrown with trees
Now almost bare of leaves?
Only the pine and cypress
Are still green. Scattered through the
Dusk are orange wild kaki on
Bare branches. Darkness, an owl
Answers the temple bell. The
Sun has passed the crosswords of
Heaven.
     There are more leaves on
The ground than grew on the trees.
I can no longer see the
Path; I find my way without
Stumbling; my heavy heart has
Gone this way before. Until
Life goes out memory will
Not vanish, but grow stronger
Night by night.
        Aching nostalgia —
In the darkness every moment
Grows longer and longer, and
I feel as timeless as the
Two thousand year old cypress.

III

The full moon rises over
Blue Mount Hiei as the orange
Twilight gives way to dusk.
Kamo River is full with
The first rains of Autumn, the
Water crowded with colored
Leaves, red maple, yellow gingko,
On dark water, like Chinese
Old brocade. The Autumn haze
Deepens until only the
Lights of the city remain.

IV

No leaf stirs. I am alone
In the midst of a hundred
Empty mountains. Cicadas,
Locusts, katydids, crickets,
Have fallen still, one after
Another. Even the wind
Bells hang motionless. In the
Blue dusk, widely spaced snowflakes
Fall in perfect verticals.
Yet, under my cabin porch,
The thin, clear Autumn water
Rustles softly like fine silk.

V

This world of ours, before we
Can know its fleeting sorrows,
We enter it through tears.
Do the reverberations
Of the evening bell of
The mountain temple ever
Totally die away?
Memory echoes and reechoes
Always reinforcing itself.
No wave motion ever dies.
The white waves of the wake of
The boat that rows away into
The dawn, spread and lap on the
Sands of the shores of all the world.

VI

Clustered in the forest around
The royal tumulus are
Tumbled and shattered gravestones
Of people no one left in
The world remembers. For the
New Year the newer ones have all been cleaned
And straightened and each has
Flowers or at least a spray
Of bamboo and pine.
It is a great pleasure to
Walk through fallen leaves, but
Remember, you are alive,
As they were two months ago.

TIM REYNOLDS

Born in Vicksburg, Mississippi in 1936, Reynolds was educated at Antioch College and Tufts, where he received a Masters in Classics, after which he lived in Japan and England, as well as San Francisco and Los Angeles. His books of poems include *Ryoanji* (1964), *Half-Life* (1964), *Slocum* (1967), *Que* (1971), *The Women Poem* (1973) and *Dawn Chorus* (1980). He moved to downtown Los Angeles in the early 1980s and lived and worked at ARCO Oil as a word processor for many years, during which he appeared in *Poetry Loves Poetry: An Anthology of L.A. Poets*. Reynolds currently lives in Long Beach.

Mommy!
F'og
B'LOOP

*   *   *

Lie-ku
I can't yet think of
a lie, not even a fib.
Whoa! It's Satori!

Two from Issa

up and down up and
down up and down up and down
mosquito larvae

*   *   *

don't swat that fly
wringing its little hands
wringing its little feet

Untitled

Oomycota
reproduce vegetative
ly by spores that swim

(zoospores) and sex
ually by male sex or
gans (antheridi-

a) and egg-produ
cing female organs (oo
gonia) developing

at the tips of the
hyphae. It wants to be in
our Gay Pride Parade.

What do we do for initials?

Recording

for Harry Partch

After the glossy vinylite whirlpool had subsided
dragging to the bottom spars flotsam buoys
sailors bottles floating crates staved-in boats
seawrack — in short after everything there was
after absolutely everything had been caught
in that amazement of water and gone down
then I found myself heaved up on a still shore
under eucalyptus and redwood trees
far from that omnivorous ocean
almost foundering again in a silence
even the shrill crickets couldn't drown.

DOREN ROBBINS

Born in Los Angeles in 1949, he lived in Santa Cruz in 1972 before returning to live there permanently in 2005. Between 1972 and 2005 he spent twenty-something years traveling, raising a family, and working as a cook and a carpenter. He lived in Oregon from 1988–1991, Iowa 1991–93, and then returned to Oregon from 1993–97. He lived in Los Angeles again from 1997–2001, teaching English and Creative Writing at East L.A. College, UCLA Extension, and Santa Monica College. From 1975–80, while primarily living in Los Angeles, he co-edited *Third Rail Journal* with Uri Hertz. Robbins' most recent collections include *Amnesty Muse* (2011), *Title to Pussy Riot* (2014) and *Twin Extra* (2015).Since 2001, he has taught at Foothill College in Los Altos Hills.

Hummingbird

Fluttering dust from his chest feathers,
I saw the shore
of white breast trim,

I saw the iridescent plum
above the white barbs.
That's what he flashed

out of apricot leaves when he aimed
his beak at two scrub jays
coming into the yard.

I think the motor sound of his wings
and his flying speed made them streak back
to the telephone wire. No fight
in those confused jays.

He likes the same apricot branch every time.
He comes here for the fire blossoms, a kind of
red honeysuckle, the juice he can't

live without, the color origin that marks him
between his heart and his throat.

Sometimes his mate flies after him
and they disappear way up
into the secreting pine.

He returns alone.

Must be he comes here to rest.
He works long hours for his abundance
and then just burns it up

flying with her, flying
into the fire blossom and back.

Bursting from his branch, he dipped all the way in,
the iridescent throat wet with honeysuckle juice,

his wings so wild with motion
the untouched red blossoms
float backward while he's there.

Tamale Place

I'm waiting for my breakfast Tamale in the Toltec.
The Saint Francis of restaurant flies blows on his plate,
moving his tongue from one corner of his mouth to the other.
He never lifts his hand, he watches the flies on his rice,
a compassionate strain tilting his lips, both eyebrows raised.

I don't know what happened to Francis or his descendants,

I don't know why we never fully believed in the Saint of Tolerance,

I don't know what happened to us.

In line in the Toltec with immigrant masons that work for shit.
A laborer wearing one stringy kneepad counted through his change.
Saint Roach stood on his back legs to examine the cherry peppers
nesting with hard-boiled eggs.

You get used to the plastic carnations.
You get used to the portrait of The Virgin smiling over crushed chili
and fruit flies.
You get used to the gas and lard smell coming out of the kitchen.

The descendants of Quetzalcoatl make the tamales.

And you can't deny it, even while the beatings go on at the border,
even while the homely Beluga, the whales of cancer,
once known as "The Canaries of the Sea"
wash up from their toxic ocean bath
on Saint Lawrence beach—you can't deny
the tamale-pleasure, because it's a lifetime

of picking up the version of the Blood Sacrifice you're born into,
and the Blood Sacrifice Language you use to get it down.

In the lucky pile of signs I talk with to myself I work
the same collective slang—a sort of pidgin Saint Francis,
a little pig Latin line-cook Don Quixote, the straightaway

language of my Blood Sacrifice.

In The Toltec in line in the morning, as if it were the Virgin of Guadalupe
I waited it out for all night. Lupe's the only one who could spice this meat.

I was safe in The Toltec, another lucky part of everything else
not bombed and poisoned flat, not homeless, not starved into the ground
at the end of that 2004 December. That's all.

I walked back with flour tortillas I couldn't finish—I served out of a bag
what I saved to the man who sat there in the day, everyday, all day,

the man grinded down to that spot, it was his corner in the day,
he was The Dayman, at his grass border, his fire hydrant, that spot,

his styllazine, prozac, demoral, xanax whatever it is
he receives to finally conk out on. I could only bring

what I saved from what I couldn't eat anymore of.
I could have just been tired of it. I couldn't even look
at what was under his nails.
Handing the food over, I smiled "the goodwill smile."
In line, in The Toltec, I admired how the Virgin bends
from her heart compliantly as though moving closer

from her calendar on the wall.

And we need her closer.
As close as she can get.

But she's not coming down from anywhere.
If you asked me about her gesture I would say you're asking about

a language that is irresistible, a language that often works in every way,
because it's the language of the illusion of comfort,

of assurance—a language out of whack
with the example of goodness,

because we shouldn't need of all things a virgin
for comfort, but a different life.

The Virgin of Guadalupe caught me
in the eyes of the woman working the counter.
She gave me "a look"

because I bickered with the guy beside me
about who was next in line—

because I had forgotten how the strands of red peppers
hang their sleeves, lapping the delicious garlic strands—

because their shaved heads bow
over the 500 Mary's of needle tracks—

because the crucifixion for the meat of tamales—

because the Saint Francis of jalapeños and flies—

because the Jesus of corn meal and lard.

Anna

Got onto the bus anyway when her third grandson's first daughter was born
in the worst heat in March since eighteen something—stepped in with all

eighty-four years of her folded green tickets to the morning and her packet
of red tickets to the evening almost used up—trundled and pushed herself

up three flights with her complaining about knees and joints of hot fluid,
supplications to the unattending but exasperatedly imagined
   grandchildren—

she was either in her forest green dress with the red and gold paisleys or the
vermillion one with the stitched on green dots under rayon silk blended

scarves with cerulean and magenta and opaque white florals, rhinestones
barnacled to her lapel and collar, cultured pearls and Woolworth

jeweled head bands and the small diamond ring no visitor to her apartment
could depart from without complimenting while she held up her hand

with a self-aware empress-like nonchalance dropped forward from her wrist
as though it was a rare exhibit, and on her hand it was a rare exhibit

because all she really knew was vanity, the charm of
transparently premeditated vanity in an old woman,

and her vanity was renown, she held forth, you believed it, her vanity
was generous not exclusive, you understood it, you were with her swathed

in her vanity, you lived beside the folds of her big body, held up
and hidden by it in the illusion of what was ultimate in yourself—willfully,

predeterminedly, as though it was a palpable substance she secreted.

In her seventies when her daughter joked and prodded her
about her older and much heavier than herself who was huge

second husband—she let out a comical insinuating laugh pounding
the palm of her hand and chanted "like a man thirty-five, darling,

like a man thirty-five..."
And that, before the fragrance past dying not yet born had begun,

and the craterous vaccinations sagged toward her thighs,
and her kelp-beds of fake jewelry were in the drawer permanently

and she cursed her God: "May he have the ears of a mouse,
may he live inside my first husband's carbuncles."

But she was enchanted in front of the crib, briefly recovered from
what started absorbing and blotting-out the stems of her voice,

the lining of her heart, her ear lobe hairs, everything. And her throat
the ten-day mouth warmed, the great-grand-daughter moving there,

breathing on the fat swell of Anna's tits rising and backstreaming,
a precious pink moth of the infant hand now waking,

wavering toward Anna, holding the face in the soiled bonnet,
chewing with lip-covered teeth the fingers and the fat arm —

shaking her head and dipping it, Anna humming,
Anna's mouth holding a plump moth, raising and shaking up

the blue rattle, the orange flame of her lipstick tinting
the child's face, the wild fluid

feeding Anna's eyes.

JOE SAFDIE

Born in Oklahoma in 1953, he grew up in Los Angeles and attended UCLA before his education began at UC Santa Cruz and, later, the University of Colorado, where he received a M.A. In the early 1980s, he was one of the co-leaders of the Venice Poetry Workshop before moving to the Bay Area, where he edited the literary magazines *Zephyr* and *Peninsula*. In the early 1990's he was a member of the Peace Corps in the former Czechoslovakia, followed by teaching jobs in Prague, Seattle and, currently, San Diego. Five chapbooks, including *September Song* (2000) and *Mary Shelley's Surfboard* (2005), were followed by the full-length collection, *Scholarship* (2014), and the forthcoming *Coastal Zone* (2015).

September Song

        (Bolinas, mid-1980s)

And now it's September in California,
almost time to gather the harvest
in this land without true season —
besides the World Series,
it's the only sign we have that autumn
has arrived, favorite theme of poetry.

But "no one listens to poetry,"
as a poet who lived in California
once wrote. And it's true, before autumn
the hope for a successful harvest
tends to dominate the daily series
of desires. It's the end of the season

in baseball, when teams rely on season-
ed veterans — or, as they're known in poetry,
Old Pros — rookies won't take you to the Series.
And only success matters in California,
which loses its glow after the harvest:
the fields turn brown, and the autumn

sun, sober, disappears at five. In *To Autumn*
Keats makes the sun and the season
seem like partners, swelling the harvest,
filling fruit with "ripeness to the core." Poetry,
though, is unappreciated in California,
where people care about being "sincere." Ease

is valued most, its price a series
of compromises that make us chilly, autumn-
al, even in spring — if California
really "sets trends," the season
that would make us responsive to poetry
hasn't dawned yet. This year's harvest

is doubtful as well, although the harvest
goddesses like the ancient Ceres
have all been appeased . . . in poetry,
at least. So we wait for the autumn
equinox, as the sun goes south for the season.
Many good citizens of California

will follow it: in California, near the harvest
moon, we say the growing season was just a series
of illusions. Say: autumn's real — not poetry.

The Poorhouse: Two Sonnets

is it the third great depression
or the Great Recession?
labels matter
"What would you say to these people?"

    (the 1.7 million unemployed
        whose benefits have been cut off)
"there's evidence that extending benefits
    will discourage the most active job search"

these miserable creatures
    addicted to the few tokes
of blighted charity
    from an ever longer and thinner pipeline

we've got to cut them off
they'll thank us in the end

*

"a pretty gloomy job picture emerged today"
    the fiscal spigots
open   not open

"short-term growth will just scare people
we can't do it in a fizzy way
    they'll know it's not real"

we have to judge the pain
    determine the quality
of the anxiety

       restore "real" confidence
  as opposed to the fake confidence
of having something to eat

some place to lay your head
America is immune to poetry

ELLEN SANDER

Born in 1944 and raised in NYC where she distinguished herself in the first wave of rock journalists, Ellen Sander moved to Bolinas in 1971 and returned to poetry. She lived there until moving to Los Angeles in 1978, where she performed readings through the 80s and 90s. In 2002, she moved to China, where she worked as an English teacher, a magazine editor and in film and TV. In 2006, she moved to Belfast, Maine and there, in 2013, was appointed to a two-year term as Poet Laureate.

DR3AM

Doctor 3 a.m.
you are the
longest hour
the haunting call of
a passing train

A buffer
before
horizon begins
its contumacious glint/pulling
that gunmetal glower
behind

I can wait/silent
unmoving
at mind's rest
not letting
expectations
tow me

After a Deluge

mist breathes out of the
loam into sunlit shafts
through overhanging branches where
chickadees fluff and a corn snake
stretches her tamarind loops
between tousled grasses
columbine bowed, lashes gleaming a
peony's lippy pout heavy with moist beading
nods

in the damp hush after the
thunder has moved on
birches still trembling
wisps of noise waft airily through
dense and luminous moisture
woodpecker's muted pocking
behind the coppice bramble, the chatter
the shimmer, the drips and the
sighs

the pond's glinted niplets
wrinkle up a mirrored sky
its carriage faster toward
the spillway, then jigging
foamy white spittle over
stones, hurls water
stumbling downstream in
an endless, skirt whirling
plunge

Four Star Review

the House nachos
were so good
i bit my finger

Daybreakage

sea smoke upriver, streetlamp
dims, the very last star drowns
in something brighter

sun, moon snarl warm
winds chill winds
circle, seething

hawks feet on carrion
poison frogs rasp the treble clef
dew on sharded jade of

eyes shuttered
my house appears
in another part of my life

daylight opens
tea falls from
steam a trickling arc

the door whines
the hasp clicks
i don't dare look

what passes for passage
misses the cup
scalding my arm

ARAM SAROYAN

Aram Saroyan was born in 1943 in New York City. After attending the University of Chicago, New York University, and Columbia, he started a literary magazine, *Lines,* in 1964. His prose books include *Genesis Angels: The Saga of Lew Welch and the Beat Generation* (1979) and a novel, *The Romantics* (1988), as well as a memoir, *Friends in the World: The Education of a Writer* (1992). His books of poetry include *Day & Night: Bolinas Poems* (1998) and *Complete Minimal Poems* (2007), which received the William Carlos Williams Award from the Poetry Society of America in 2008. *Door to the River: Essays and Reviews from the 1960s into the Digital Age* was published in 2010. He taught for many years at the University of Southern California.

Friendly Persuasion

The body and the mind
Have a talk together

And the mind convinces the body
To go out with it on a date.

Soon afterwards
The mind calls the body up on the telephone

And says,
"Why don't you drop by?"

"When?" the body asks.
"How 'bout this afternoon."

In no time at all the mind and the body
Are going steady.

Then they get married.
For a while they are very poor

And sometimes they have to go and stay at the body's folks' place
And then they have to stay at the mind's folks' place.

Neither one is a very good place to stay
They decide

And almost immediately they have a child.

The Mind Is a Medium

The mind is a medium
And delights in its own movement,
Disclosures, gestures.

It has a style
For every man, woman, and child;
An alphabet of forms that is

Literally
Inexhaustible. What could not be seen
Within the mind's roving, restless

Eye? An expressionist
As deep as Van Gogh; a minimalism
That contracts

And expands into multiples of its
Own perfect
Nothingness: this mind is pastel

At times,
Chiaroscuro in other, fiercer
Moments, and can be reduced to

The raging
Scribbles of a forlorn child.
But this mind is a stylist, too.

Its view, a river;
Or a knife and fork
To proportion any meal

Set before it. Or else
The laughing mind,
Letting rhythm loosen

Its sphere into
Comedies of manners,
Mores, Mondays, and moths.

An alliterative wonderer,
A wanderer of summer
Mornings, alluded to moods of

Remembered con-
Versations with a plant? What will it
Not go through to sustain

The rapid answering, the listless
Inquiring—a chemical circus
In the extreme;

And yet
The deepest, clearest pool
This mind also is;

As if it had been cosmically
Checked, righted like a tie
In a mirror: a God's eye view

Of itself in the cosmos.

The Moment

The moment is like this. Suddenly you *see*. The words are gone; the vision is absolutely empty of the usual interior monologue that accompanies our daily round. It might be anything. An oil stain on a rain-soaked pavement. A tree in sunlight. A shoulder; a handkerchief; a tricycle.

Part of the seeing is not knowing what is being seen; not knowing, that is, in the ordinary sense of knowing it by naming it. Instead, one is seeing with a complete attention that transcends the names — exceeds them, outspeeds them.

There it is, suddenly: nothing.

Nothing is misunderstood. It is the name given to what goes beyond simple naming.

Because the seeing here is more than the object seen; the seeing is an action in which the see-er and seen commingle to the degree of losing one another as separate, discrete identities. They merge, and in merging are one (moving) thing.

This nothing is — and is — and is.

Until the name occurs.

Sweater, say. Or orange.

Stopping it. Giving the name ends the dance: the verb is replaced by a noun.

*

This kind of seeing is beauty, too, perhaps even in the precise sense that Keats meant it in his "Beauty is truth, truth beauty." For in the end might not the beautiful be defined as whatever empties the mind, causing the seeing to become pure, mirror-like?

The act of a mirror is self-dispossession. Consciousness.

*

Lew Welch, speaking of poets, once said that the suicide misses by just a quarter of an inch. What he meant, I think, is that self-dispossession is the source of poetry — but the act of the poet is to die *into* the world, not out of it.

A Dream

I dreamed I found out
Death was no big deal
No more really
Than a kind of invisible membrane
You walk through
To the other side of the day
The same kind of thing
As lets a mouse know
A person just opened his eyes in the room
In the middle of the night
So the mouse stops making noise
And it was such a relief to know it
I was walking along
And the sun was shining
When it got through to me
And a great weight seemed to lift
From my heart
I felt warm and happy and courageous
As if everything were possible
And the world was a perfect situation

STANDARD SCHAEFER

Born in 1971 in Houston, Texas, Standard Schaefer moved to Los Angeles, in 1991, to attend Occidental College, where he studied under Martha Ronk and Douglas Messerli. There he wrote his first book of poetry *Nova*, which was selected for the 1999 National Poetry Series and published by Sun & Moon Books. His second book, *Water & Power*, was published in 2005, when he moved to San Francisco and then wrote *Desert Notebook* (2008) and *The Notebook of False Purgatories* (2013). In 2010, he moved to Portland, Oregon, where he currently lives with his wife and daughter. He has co-edited several literary and arts journals including *Ribot, New Review of Literature, Rhizome, The Feralist* and *Or*.

from *Water & Power*

Bride of gunpowder, caviar, and benzodiazepines, she said
"Liberty is an elephant swimming towards Kansas," her voice
with the French corners cancelled the capricious crag of the sky
but flipping through her easter pages, exposed corners swirl of leaves
and a constant laying on of the hands—

*

Through the slit in the attic,

lots and fixed forms,
        sleet, crickets

one who plays with marbles
one who conducts a vague science

a slow escalation—
in living only as well as one breathes

against the reclamation of dust, a desert
salvaged from dust by the mildest powders the longest valley
wind through the synapse whispers glimmers dreaming east of Lone Pine

the trees there flutter like porchlights on the grasses of Ohio
were it ever Ohio were there trees
thin as grass if there is any grass left anywhere
in this hopped-up sauna room on this horse-shaped continent
amid the city born corrupt, that is to say, capacious

*

But I blame moonbeams and a mouse that met on a train
for hiring the man in the powder blue suit, after which
the one with the pen seemed to have the least to do
given his ration of talent to pillowy cloud, and a rabid anti-socialism
reflected in a nature film about VD and walking off with an Academy award

even Old Ez watched Uncle Walt whenever he need to catch up
on some serious foot dangling

but how long can an empire depend on a distracted child
how many hours extra on the exam given the custom
of being born into it and choosing instead to write
not exactly highly selected letters about the destruction of California
long overdue like relatives and residuals still crawling
off them mountains

with a bouquet of bayonets and a penchant
for banquets they came down "to see the elephant"

on this burdened archipelago of bad options and enthusiasms.

North of Lone Pine, East of Independence

the land leaking from the land dry lightning cut
glass in the sand a nation of almost no imagination
fields an army of engines give only no for an answer
each grain a riddle of error or Nevada but out of Nevada
the answer is saw dust in the veins and even the *alcalde*
is willing to admit all he remembers is names and dates
nerves of dirt for a sense of direction but even hurricanes
have pangs of property and learned to stay away out of a healthy regard
for the right to stray and nothing is something there's plenty of
what leaves as what returns patterns in bone two or three degrees
above sleep or the next valley where they plant mercury
lead and arsenic hoping each day the knuckles stiffen
a little less the mouth hardly open despite centipedes
        scorpions and Indians
the soft whip of deduction gone drowsily pragmatic
reaches the conclusion anything with motion has to be wet.

The Forties or the Mountains No One Talks About

begins or does not at forty or in the movies with or without gold or legal age
whether or not war is work for all always with Diamond Lil there is work
her falsetto heels across the floorboards Spanish trickling in from the dais
a kind of provocation to the violin gradually consuming the lanai or a climate
built on gunpowder and smeared over the eyes like Rita Hayworth
high on velvet or was that the girl painted on the background of the check
who leased her eyes to the city of Ojai or perhaps it was another Miranda
     altogether
who true to the rites of spring took her guns strictly bullets first
and from there was shipped east and west at once by Colonel Capra
and the Hollywood Canteen to cough out an alibi no brighter or better than Ojai
or Odessa, daisy after daisy the sky black with ducks when Disney against
the metaphysic asked to sit this one out in Casablanca like a brand of beer
like troutfat and hard freight like minor song brought out to defeat more recent
arrivals such as twelve-tone music and a cresting fluorescence concealed and
     embodied
in the punch-line to the fishing guide's joke that he don't mind reading
but only for knowledge
       the valley returning to its lush sheep-like devastation relies
very sparingly on the reel or Veronica Lake and opening day but
knows damn well that with an airport this town it could be as big as Laredo
so is willing to abide questions and interviews that all boil down
to whether or not he is impotent but the only way to avoid impotence, sincerity
or Hollywood, as Stravinsky said, is to live there once and for all.

The Airplane Graveyard of Mojave

Fat on suicides and cluttered with lead balloons
the kiss-my-axle hurly-burly of flies not rising
from blocks of light, knots of mirage siphoning off
the sound of muffled bees reminds the director
of certain eastern spiders but ever buoyant
rarely embarrassed the cadavers in the voting box
cast shadows on the concrete and concrete keeps coming
hard the heat keeps still and the fat keep voting the dead

The L.A. River

smog typhoid celery like a ghost splashing out of a beaker
comes a dot off the ridge to cancel the orthography
of bramble and pine the abyss fits in the parenthesis
fragrance of isotherms route numbers and the glint in the chrome
that hits the vein each day more prophylactic than the exit wound
of pragmatism and public work but with a plush silence
has no preference though if pushed hedges with performance
dim pleats in the slovenly limits of custom obligation verve
works the work of the major languish against slobber, skin, and
any serviceable language of submission and proposal
come and gone in spars and shafts part e-flat part pleas
twelve chords of gray ash until sixty watts off shore
it does nothing but at least it does it consistently, despite
shortness of breath and the liver's long career of whispering yes

MICHAEL SHEPLER

Born in Ohio, and raised in Los Angeles, Shepler was a student in Henri Coulette's writing workshops at California State University, Los Angeles. He had a play produced by the legendary Company Theater in Los Angeles in 1980 and had poems in the anthology, *Poems of the American West* (2002). He currently lives in San Francisco. His books of poetry include *The Barbara Payton Story* (1988), *Angel's Flight: New and Selected Poems* (1995), and *Blue Lanterns* (2002).

Harvey Apartments, Santa Monica Blvd

When the night clerk closed the registration book
A speck of dust flew up his nose.
Extracting a gray handkerchief, he blows
As if he hoped to clear his head,
Erasing all thought of those who've crossed his path.

Past midnight. He's processed the last guest.
Sedated as an asylum, the hotel's quiet.
Beyond the lobby's wilderness, the walls possess a watchfulness.

Bliss quickens in that furnished bower,
A kind of love, or its counterfeit;
A flower in a death-house vase.
The ecstatic scaffolding collapses.
Such eerie music pervades this place.

(6/9/14)

Requiem

(For Anna Ahkmatova)

The shadow of a microphone
in the overhead light. . .

You put your finger to the lips
as if to blow our visitor a kiss,
then point first to the ceiling,
and then the walls,
a wistful shadow in a shawl.

A shadow of a microphone
in the overhead light.
An indiscretion? even a poem?
Whisper of an open line.

In the years of Yezhov
and prison queues. . .

whisper of a hidden wire.
Mute listener;
sleepless listener through implacable night.

"Would you like some tea"
How sunburned you are!
Autumn is so early this year!"
Idle talk about the evening star.

Rapidly scribbling on a scrap of paper
and handing it to Lidia.
The words reach deep into the mind,
the memory of Lidia,
your single reader.
The match flares,
is touched against
the scrap.
The edges of the paper blacken, curl.

The cars outside sounding very like
cars in far Brazil.
Shadowy figures linger beneath lamp-posts.
Their black jackets crackle,
the strap of their shoulder holsters, visible.

Angel's Flight

For Jackie

Gold evening light streams through the window,
falling on the bed where the fallen angels lie,
having loved.

It streams through my fingers,
it touches your face.

Funicular light,
descending, ascending,
growing faint with the rush of night.

Behind my eyes, a disconnected image,
snapshot of Bunker Hill —
vanished, mythic as an Arabian night.
the tiny cars of Angel's Flight.

A Windy Night

Waking from dreams into windswept night
I rise slowly and move
down the unlighted hall
to the kitchen, the door
through to the porch
and yard beyond
where a picket of trees stand guard;
and the moon has risen
a cameo crescent
beaten by the wind
bordered by the shuddering leaves
of an ancient oak.

JACK SPICER

Born in Los Angeles in 1925, where he grew up, he graduated from Los Angeles
High School and then attended the University of Redlands, east of the city. In
1945 he moved to Berkeley to study at the university, where he would begin a
life-long friendship with Robin Blaser and Robert Duncan. He left his graduate
studies in linguistics at UC Berkeley in 1950, rather than take the infamous
California "loyalty oath" required of all teaching assistants, as well as full-
time faculty. After moving around for several years, from Minneapolis and
the University of Minnesota, and later sojourns in New York and Boston, he
returned to San Francisco in 1956, where he would remain until his death in
1965. In that ten-year period, starting with the groundbreaking *After Lorca*
(1957), Spicer would publish some of the most important work in post-War
American poetry, including *The Heads of the Town up to the Aether* (1962),
Language (1965) and the posthumous *Book of Magazine Verse* (1966). In 1975, the
Collected Books of Jack Spicer appeared, edited by Robin Blaser, and in 2009, *My
Vocabulary Did This to Me: The Collected Poetry of Jack Spicer*, edited by Peter
Gizzi & Kevin Killian.

Apollo Sends Seven Nursery Rhymes to James Alexander

I.

You have not listened to a word I have sung
Said Orpheus to the trees that did not move
Your branches vibrate at the tones of my lyre
Not at the sounds of my lyre.
You have set us a tough problem said the trees
Our branches are rooted in fact to the ground
Through our trunks said the trees
But calm as an ax Orpheus came
To the trees and sang on his lyre a song
That the trees have no branches the trunks have no tree
And the roots that are gathered along
Are bad for the branches the trunk and the tree
Say, said the trees, that's a song
And they followed him wildly through rivers and oceans
Till they ended in Thrace with a bang.

II.

At the La Brea Tar Pits
There is a sheer drop then twenty feet of stars. I
Believe this occasionally.
The white skeletons
Jammed in there in the black tar
Don't come back
Can't
Come back
No ghosts
Only occasionally
Ronnie.

The mouse ran up the chessboard
The mouse ran down the chessboard
He destroyed:
> two pawns and a queen and bit a hell of an edge
  off a black rook
Savage
As the god of plague is savage
Apollo the mouse ran up the chessboard
Down the chessboard.

IV.

Or, explaining the poem to myself, Jay Herndon has only three
words in his language
Door: which means that he is to throw something which will
make a sound like a door banging.
Fffish: which means that there is something that somebody showed him
And Car: which is an object seen at a great distance
He will learn words as we did
I tell you, Jay, clams baked in honey
Would never taste as strange.

I died again and was reborn last night
That is the way with we mirror people

Forgive me, I am a child of the mirror and not a child of the door.

Yes, Apollo, I dare. And if the door opens

North of the North Wind

V.

A Christmas toy misdirected, a baseball game, A
Stounding Science Fiction
All this, but the eyes are full
Of tears? of visions? of trees?
So close to nonsense
That there could be a hand, a throat, a thigh
So close to nonsense that the mind shuttles
Between
The subway, station of what would'
Nt.

vi. The Death of Arthur

Pushing wood, they call it when you make automatic moves in a chess game
or in
    a poem
Pushing tar
The sound, the subway, the skeleton of the whole
    circumstances you and everybody else was born with
The dance (that you do whenever Apollo or any other smaller god is not
watching
    you) the dance
Of probability
Be-
    ing human.

VII.

Fire works
But like the bottom of an alley
They works only
With people in them.
Justly suspicious
Jay did not like the sparks flying past his head
Although they were blue green yellow and purple
And several also made a big whhupp.
Fire works
Broken words
But never repairing
Jay, justly suspicious,
Afterwards
Said, "Fffish"

JOHN THOMAS

Born as John Thomas Idlet in Baltimore, Maryland, in 1930. After serving in the U.S. Air Force in the early 1950s, and fathering two families, he hitchhiked to California from Texas in 1959 and by chance ended up in Venice, California rather than his destination, San Francisco. Inspired by the Venice West scene, he began writing poetry, then moved to San Francisco in the early 1960s, where he wrote his best early work and began publishing it in magazines such as *kayak, Floating Bear* and *Evergreen Review.* He moved back to Los Angeles in 1965 and lived there for the remainder of his life. He died on March 29, 2002. His books of poems include *John Thomas John Thomas* (1972), *Epopoeia and the Decay of Satire* (1976), *Abandoned Latitudes* (with Robert Crosson & Paul Vangelisti, 1983), and *The Selected Poems and Prose of John Thomas* (2011), edited by Pegarty Long.

Tarquin

> "it is snail today about
> 4 whorls in the ice on the
> Arctic floe southerly"

—EILEEN IRELAND

"The first thing, to do violence to your myths/
to be your own
Tarquin..." said almost without thought, his attention
on the barbed wire, as I held it up for him
and he climbed through.
There were patches of snow on the yellow grass, still
But they would be gone by evening

      (Lucretia! were the breasts
      marble? And the throat
      did it pulse then? Let the snow melt   enough
      that I had loved it

It was a pig farm, and no way around it/
garbage and tin cans in the mud, the pigs
glancing at us from under their eyelashes/
Bill with his eyes watching where his feet stepped
among the stinking tress   I think
He never stopped talking

      (the surgeons would carry canes, and in the heads of the canes
      cloves, rosemary, other scents to breathe
      as they walked through the wards

Through the fence on the other side
then a stream   we took off our shoes and waded across
the water so cold my feet ached/
and what he had said to the American girl at the Louvre
the girl who had come over to write novels about Boston
and that she lived with a psychopathic Russian
who beat her and who pretended not to understand English
and what the Russian and he (Bill) had done to the girl
in a doorway by Notre Dame
and afterwards all three in the bed

which was probably a lie, although you could never be sure, with Bill

All easy going now, low hills and dirt roads/
on the barn door two stretched coonskins
also an owl with the wings nailed out   a rusty
harrow behind the barn

       (lists. And maps of backcountry where no one
       walks any more. Is there anything else to make?

A windrow of Lombardy poplars
which we followed up the millrace
to the dam and the graves

I tied a string to the wine bottle
then lowered it into the green water of the dam
all the way down to the bottom   there were
huge treetrunks and old tires down there
the mud was very still/
while the wine was chilling we examined the graves

three families only
mostly children's stones
but the ones who had gotten through childhood had lived
—ninety-four years old, ninety-eight, a hundred and four/
Bill silent now   just our feet
on the brittle weeds, and a woodpecker somewhere in the trees behind us/
one fine stone, six-by-three, set flat in the dirt

William J Perkins
1791-1888
Last Survivor
Of The
Maryland Defenders

(that would be Fort McHenry or the Battle of North Point)
upon which we ate the lunch   we had brought
a provolone cheese, bread, a fine red onion, oranges
and the bardolino, which was cold now
         (lists. And rubbings from tombstones
         and how cold the wine was. Is there
         anything else, now? Anything more
         now, three years later, letters from

that country telling me that Bill thinks
of little but suicide? Only the lists come back
and maps of tombstones and of dry hills
—anything more is merely
possible

(Lucrece! The throat, did it pulse?
and was the grief real, or poetical only?
there, see   the snow melts
and the grass is yellow underneath

the book had been in his pocket. Goethe, and he
read   "Whoever works with symbols only is a pedant,
        a hypocrite, or a bungler. There are many such,
        and they like to be together. Their babbling
        detains..."

for coming back we chose a different way, did not
wade the stream/
he was quiet, breathing heavily because of the hills/
certainly the graves are still there
and we had thrown the wine bottle into the dam, watched it
sink, so it
remains

the weather here is different
the children   are brown, have
never seen snow
so everything is different/
I, Tarquin, sit in the afternoon sun
making lists
drawing maps of that realm
all else now is
merely possible.

Variations on the Decay of Satire

for Taylor Mead

I

Most gentle of duelists, you asked: "Why brandish the sword so,
before the thrust?" then passed on to other things,
me perhaps the only one who saw the flashing blade;
now, therefore, a parry with the wrist, in the Italian manner
and no riposte, only the twist that essays to disarm:

2

it is simply this, man: we lack opponents, could only
fight each other, and to what end two good blades shattered?
a mutual killing? no,
in these quiet times the samurai becomes a tea man,
builds temple gardens, floats plum blossoms
in a shallow bowl before the image. . .

3

it is the times;
one has inherited this wax museum —
ten cents for a walkaround, see the
heroes, see the famous murders, see here Charlotte Corday
in dusty chiffon bending over the famous bathtub
and Marat's vital blood melting, now, from the faulty furnace —
it is the times, Taylor. I had hoped
for a better legacy, but must be the curator of this one with good grace.

4

Or consider it from the inside, as structure:
see the mind lunging, no sabre now,
without the linear precision of the fencing strip,
but as through a thicket, simply away from
the center, inattentive to symmetry —
building holes in the rain forest,
stumbling over treetrunks in the green shadows —
Conquistador! you crossed the Andes, headed east, and the dagger
rusted among rivers that lost themselves in mud and breast-high weeds —
it is the times, Conquistador, and the structure:
twenty years' paid service in the Italian wars, siege of Milan,
pitched battles from end to end of that unhappy peninsula,
had not prepared you for these dripping slopes.

The good steel becomes red powder in its sheath,
And only the Spanish shape of mind is useful now,
Only that willfulness and melancholy vanity that say,
"There, where the dead horse lies, will be the Church of St. Jude,
and there, by the sour pond, the market place. . . ."
and make it so.

5
And, finally—
it is the times, Taylor, and the shifting of the image on its base.
We have seen so much blood.
The corpses mock us—we stink of our victories.
And there is this secret we share:
one of them rode up the center of the street,
gun strapped low, brave in the summer sun,
and in the subsequent blur of fear and fatigue
we shot him. Dead brave face in the dust of the street
—and he was the wrong man.
That was the time to turn in the badge and move on,
take up farming or run freight to Silver City
—because, you see, he was the wrong man, and after him
we're always wrong. So do not tempt me, Taylor.
I have retired from that trade.
I have set my mind to building a basilica. . . .

PAUL VANGELISTI

Paul Vangelisti is the author of some twenty books of poetry, as well as being a noted translator from Italian. His most recent book is *Wholly Falsetto with People Dancing* (2013), an older man's not-so-divine comedy. From 1971-1982 he was co-editor, with John McBride, of the literary magazine *Invisible City* and, from 1993-2002, edited *Ribot*, the annual report of the College of Neglected Science. He worked as a journalist at the *Hollywood Reporter* (1972-1974), and as Cultural Affairs Director at KPFK Radio (1974-1982). Currently, with Luigi Ballerini & Gianluca Rizzo, he is editing a six-volume anthology of U.S. poetry from 1960 to the present, *Nuova poesia americana*, for Mondadori in Milan. Vangelisti was Founding Chair of the Graduate Writing program at Otis College of Art & Design and is now a professor in that program.

Azusa: a Sequel

for Wallace Berman & Stuart Z. Perkoff

Another porch light left on, another way back, exacting, shimmering along the bone. Another ox or angel, another appetite so grand its arithmetical value is 1.

Busted, cracked, the mirror just inside the front door: lost voices on a radio, intermittent ticking and scratching, even a daybreak hillside peacock shriek sometimes leaking through the surface. An easy sound, an entrance no longer there.

C or *gimel*, with an arithmetical value of 3, where optimists abound willing to arrange anybody's camel. He slides a hand along the wall feeling for the switch, then stops, waits for the darkness to ring.

Does it divide or simply declare a "warm source, where we suckle and worship"? A door we must move through, as you say, with "the fact of our abundant flesh," its arithmetical value rhyming with 4?

Every day almost the winds move as breath across the city, from west to east, to the steep arroyo above the river. A drift and stir, whose value is five, an occasional troubling of the waters.

Five minutes have passed when our subject reappears, flopping behind the wheel and then gone, downhill. Five senses, balancing revelation, whose arithmetical number is 6.

Given seven cracked mirrors, a gaunt heart enameled bravissimo, the eyes of the dead, the clamor of snow, our harvest moon speaks but once and hardly means it.

Hunger for movement, a stolen bone in the maws of energy. An hour, unlike ours, that must always come, a plight more venture than romance, in a biz makes audience of us all and Hamlet of a well-hung Polonius.

Is the most impolitely hermetic in the system, in the yawn from hand to I. Silly bird in the sky, is it a marvel pointing, a history of talking mostly about oneself?

Keeping a hand half-closed, hollow of the hand translated from Semitic tool to symmetrical *kappa*; question following like a perfumed skin or moth to sleep. Its arithmetical value is 20.

Linking arms and wings, an extension of the sky herself, despite those acoustics of time. Phone any latitude you might, you will probably find laughter, cousin or father.

Maybe it's the water, as once it spelled mother, in a capital of lunatics, whose whispering spills the dashes tricking one to sleep. Water-mother, dribbling a faint smile on our melodrama she doesn't forget.

No obstacles, but a burning leaving it all behind. Grandfather, father, son, a progress, a hunger, disoriented and finally symmetrical. Fish, by any other name, that makes finicky escort; its arithmetical number is 50.

O, smallest of any sign in the writing: a noise, a jumble, an old heart with an oar, a chaos trapped inside the head, echoing the eye fed in a stormy circle.

Pe or *pei*, meaning mouth, open mouth, creature of repetition. Until near the start one loots the decision and the dead find esoteric clime to preen like arrows shot in reverse. Purpose (or is it living) makes for such a poor tool.

Question is, impaled on the hook of god, what doesn't seem to be an answer or even much of a question. Just a history of rocks, of emptiness and terror: the oldest monkey in the book. Its arithmetical value is 100.

Reversing its head, as we perceived it, before it was aroused and rowed ashore. Is the purer clime, like music, already housed in your wilderness? Who can wait?

So it was named the *tooth*, with its "impelling music," as you called it, "gowned! perfumed! jeweled! A sweet rhyme eternal." Beauty and truth, a snake if there ever was one, with an arithmetical value of 300.

There it goes, there it goes, there it goes, and ever the wrong tempo. Who might tolerate or even sever the hand you cannot kiss, if offered nightly on the wind. One grows tired, here and there, of translation.

Victory doesn't deserve the question, since a person plays the piano, the good doctor claims, for the same reason a spider spins webs. Six may be its arithmetical number but it was love ate the red wheelbarrow.

X, you explained, became a slithering hiss echoing through our cosmos. Unripe, my X's knelt like alphabets in your snow, growing remorseful of the future. Then again, who's plain skittish in the duty of your abrupt school, when value is bound for X?

"Zounds!" you exclaim, "must be Azusa, the old A-Z in the U.S.A." Zero, zip, nada, almost a perfect start, as the blue hour outcries the earth rotating under us, and Z, not X, marks the spot.

from *Days Shadows Pass*

20
Which seems the unlikeliest beginning
so far and reticent as a hawk wheeling
in arroyo light, a new word old world
occasionally palpable as verses.
Or to turn again so far back that this
dream or dying of language suspended
over an uncertain low terrain, lavender
lavender, dead language giving more life
to thought. So far back let's cross out hope
again deep in windless wordless earth our
view of language separated by language.
And has a dictionary enough Sundays
enough reason to overbalance us
halve us or have us dream as we are?
Weaving the dialects in these hilly acres
of wind and quiet not necessarily
the death of words corresponds to the lull
of ocean and mountains, long valleys of sighs
and begetting, lonely bird-faced man in love with
everybody save his own. Lavender is
where it waits, no arch, pediment or pale
just the merest garden in a whisper
of characters, a kindly kindling
of breath fluttering each way. Linger a while,
Bob, like a winter's dream of Catalina,
Come and take me slowly in your blank heart.

21
Undoubtedly feminine or masculine, blue violet
or lavender, fraught with the optimism of dear dead
grandmothers and grandfathers coming down the hill.
The legend is rather simple: promises hidden
among the many topical symbols and notations,
O Riccia Riccia, of diminishing territory.
And us all such bad actors we make a place to wear out
the earth so as poverty and sin be silent. Tarnation
it be a wicked body grow symbols on every street
corner standing for profit and loss. And the rest wait

for retirement to return (for a small consideration)
to the scene of whatever crime isn't yet crawling with
knives and forks and anything but food on the table.
But what pays, reminded Black Bart at the gates of
San Quentin disappearing forever from history, is not
the crime of poesy but flying obsessively lower
until everything on the screen resembles a landscape
with barely a heartbeat. Here we are coming to an end
and if the pendulum hasn't quite stopped it surely trembles
lucid in the forgetful wind that is always the king's wind.

25
Listen, not everybody is so obvious
or forlorn, I'm a stranger here myself
indifferent to many things but gardening,
looking to get in or out of an almost
astonishing sum of living along
the same old thirsty river. Otherwise
hallelujah to what isn't always.
A kiss may cloud your memory depending
on how comfortable your daddy and
or his people from Texas or Oklahoma
or someone who has heard even more stories
about a soft green dress whispered backwards
outside a café you went back to
every day, regardless of the popsicles,
peppermint, shipwreck and tiny umbrellas
in your cocktail, a feint smell of cordite,
flashing palms, then sunshine and bandages.
Sentences have nothing to do with it.
Reluctance can't matter much with no hint
of rain or a name of any woods besides.
Gardeners sport evening dress or overalls
for those who want to reassess anything
like post-modernism or modernism
so why keep practicing desolation?
Push for a sequel, trust the zeal of the amazon
or anything hilly without beginning or end.

SCOTT WANNBERG

Born in Santa Monica in 1953, Wannberg attended Venice High School and eventually moved to San Francisco, where in 1977 he earned an M.A. from San Francisco State University. He moved back to Los Angeles and worked at Brentwood Bookstore, which would become Dutton's Books in Brentwood, where Wannberg achieved legendary status as book clerk and buyer until the iconic store's closing in 2008. He toured the United States and Canada with poetry-performance ensembles *The Carma Bums* (1989-2009), *New Word Order* (2005), *The Deciders* (2006) and *Sal Mimeo & The Revolution Without Applause* (2007). His books include *Mr. Mumps* (1982); *The Electric Yes Indeed!* (1989); *Strange Movie Full of Death* (2009); and *Tomorrow Is Another Song* (2011). He died in 2011 in Florence, Oregon. Wannberg's 306-page, posthumous collection, *The Official Language of Yes*, edited by S.A. Griffin, was published by Perceval Press in 2015.

from *the cat put me out last night just before world war* III *came strutting down my street to angrily knock on my door and demanded that i tell it what the hell i meant when i gave my dog my car keys and said here, you take care of business for awhile*

1

who invented the murder?
who sold the country?
once again the sleeping mirages
poked their noses
into the sundown
calypso

once again the meandering murmurs
of not that contented people
plying their hurt trade
in the vital spotlight
of the dark eye of
night

who invented the orange juice?
who shot the mayor down in cold blood?
who invented the switch blade and called it god?
once again the helicopters
around and around in the stomach of sky
go for it
with their noise and lights
reminding me of the blind
spot that love has for
the just

2

on account of
because of
the reason stated thus so explicable and culpable in
hideaway areas of demented brains passing for sanity in
oh them squalor rid hovels of the heart gone mad and blown
sideways in the Sunday Supplement Section (see this new house
on the beautiful virgin hill? Bricks and a fence and a gate
and a dog that kills. You will NOT BE TOUCHED)
on account of
because of
the freebies and fresno freedom fighters

3
doing freebies in the funny farm of
mankind. dusting off the incriminating finger things
from the smoking smoldering murder thing i
heard the Governor spit up blood and do his dance on the
neck of the electric chair and said
See See See Dan White is a White Man
Dan White is A White Man is A White Man is A White Man

4
Okay fucking Twinkie
defense okay Dan White kills Moscone
Milk does it real funky bang a bang a bang
two people with their San Francisco blood on the carpet
(hey hey hey) the fucking Twinkie Case

5
Dan White
White man
ex-cop
conservative dresser
wanted his gig back
he carried a gun into City Hall that morning
sweet of him
he killed the mayor of S.F.
he killed the mayor in his office
and then proceeded as if nothing had happened to
the office of the Supervisor Harvey Milk and then
shot him too (hey hey hey)
in cold blood with the same gun
he used on Mr. Moscone
and the
guilty party
in it all
were Twinkies

6
I ate a Twinkie
I killed my brother
I ate a Fig Newton
I killed my sister
I ate a chocolate chip cookie
I killed a cab driver

Dan White taught me how you do it
tonight tomorrow
right even now

7
I wanna go home the dead guy said
I wanna be put back together like I used to seem
In the tired morgue hallway
the butlers and the maids
sing and croon and do the dusty steps
as the evening eavesdrops on
the lonely motels in the mind
as the tired killers are sick
of being tired killers in this wonderful
wonderful world

8
The guard with the hands that kill
Aimed his rifle at the moon and wished he were a God
You can get by sometimes doing shit like that. Sometimes.

9
Angry motherfucks
doing time on the ground where I grew
my garden this year as the gang members of this turf cut
down the jugulars of the gang members of that turf. Oh the
territory of a dog
raising his leg to pee and the
smells of the carbon copy going up going down
The victim, a Male Negro
The victim, a Male Caucasian
The victim, a Male Hispanic
The victim, a Female Negro
the victim, a a a a a a A is for Atlanta
A is for Apple, A is for Albacore, A is for Finally Albatross
hanging around the hung low rock neck of the night

gods shooting pool at Vasquez's parlor where the Dirty Fucking
Deal Went down Finally
they paid for O'Meara's body
they paid for Shimatsu's neck
they paid for Lowenstein's arms
the dirty fucking deal in the hospital corridor where they

put the incriminating medicine into his sleeping eye as
the Arabs arm wrestled the Jews, as the IRA blew up the trees
in London
as the Night went sleepwalking
with Twinkies all along the border

10
I have a vision, someone said, in the projection room
I will go there and free those people, someone else said and
the hand of time reached down across the buffet table and closed
gentle upon the tired memories of the day.

11
the cat put me out last night, mother
just before World War III came strutting
down my street to angrily
knock on my door and demanded that I tell it
what the hell I meant when I gave my dog
my car keys and said Here, you take
care of business for awhile

12
the business we be is the business we take care of

13
We don't know why Dan White came to L.A.
Darryl Gates said and kicked his foot against the moon
We don't know why he came here
We most certainly don't need him here
We have enough trouble with Twinkies as it is

14
Asleep
the receding
feet of dreams
forming dance steps along some
soft carpet of
the brain

21
I believe in the world.
Come and sing.
Against this cold night

light. Against this
street of fear. Come
and I will play my music
until they throw us out.
Come and believe in the world.
I believe in the world

I believe in the world

I believe.

MAW SHEIN WIN

Born in Massachusetts in 1963, Maw Shein Win studied creative writing at California State University, Long Beach in the 1980s. In 1983, she started a zine called *Lemon Fingers Emerge*, which included work by Southern California poets such as Amy Gerstler, Gerald Locklin, Nichola Manning, and David Trinidad. She moved to the Bay Area in the mid-90s and co-founded a literary and arts journal, *Comet*, with Kathleen Munnelly. Presently she is a poetry editor for *Rivet: The Journal of Writing that Risks*.

A bed with softer animals

It is raining.
It is Tuesday night.
There are 36 steps up to Alan's apartment on the East Side.
A bed with softer animals.
A Doberman Pinscher walks into a 7-11 and buys a carton of milk.
I notice these things.

Rain waters the buildings and they grow and grow.
Makes thieves work harder.
Softens mountains.
Ruins sandwiches.

Some paintings make me cry.
I Like Crying.
Gunsmoke was a good show to cry to.
Also, the *Waltons' Christmas Special.*

Alan is reading about cannibals in New Guinea.
The cannibals average at five feet tall.
They roast their dead for 30 days then bury them in the jungle.
Alan told me it rains more in the jungle, but I knew that already.

What I don't know is how lightning feels on the body.
Or what makes a glowworm glow.
Or why the neighbor keeps knocking his head against the wall.

Five days in a city

The houseplant moved on its own volition across the planked floor.
Trails of laughing beetles.
An eye. An egg. A riverbed.

Twins growing in the belly of her niece.
Imprint. Cyclic.
Gingko leaves spilling from trees in front of brick facades.

The grandmother adorned in costume jewelry sips
from a flask of brandy in the morning.
The mother holds her arm up high,

an unlit match in her hand.
Broken, she tells her children. *Your arms are broken, too.*
We're going to hospital.

Sunken cheeks of models, tiny birds fallen out of nests.
A paper boat adrift on a lake. She considers forgiveness.
A woman on crutches curses the lack of elevators in the subway station.

Six maple trees and a flattened starflower in a silver frame.

the farm without name

the home of claude cahun and suzanne malherbe

she longs for her stepsister's hips
she counts the crumbs in her lover's house
she clutches at feathers with no regrets
she remains several women
she is a masked gymnast
she wipes off the sweat while no one looks
she is the heart of a woodpecker
she is a farm without name
she longs for her stepsister's hips with half-closed eye and shuttered lens.

he picks the syllables up off the floor
he is a braided girl
he has never heard of the isle of jersey
he is a constructor and explorer of objects he lives alone on the eighth floor
he is afraid to leave
he has green eyes like fresh weeds
he is squandered and condemned
he is a farm without name
he picks the syllables up off the floor and tosses them into the air again.

it slides to the ground
it fills empty jars
it rests in the shade
it grasps at linen bolts
it is paris in the winter
it is constant as a cat
it is the mania of the exception it is the public gaze
it is a farm without name
it slides to the ground with its palms face up.

the collective dreams of mice

i.
the ranch hand sitting on the horse looking bored as a rabbit
they fought at the wedding but the bride didn't notice
the sun shot a glance at the satellite circling the city
a breathing and impervious endive
an imploring and shifty senator

ii.
the mice under the house
trapped in the steel wool
envision the oxeye daisies
tracing the hills
the hours last for hours

iii.
in gokarna the swedes gather
in pomona the greeks lather
and, in the end, they call it a day

Score

The film score is a Turkish bathhouse, a thankless accountant, a back country road in Montana, a shy teenager, a loving aunt, a wine glass with a painting of a cow on it, the underbelly of a cat, a stream running along the outside of a prison, the shadow of an orchid, a heroin addict, a blanket statement, a lemon rolling down the hill, a blister on the tip of a finger, a forest ranger, a chunk of ice melting, a bully, a bowl of fresh honey, an abandoned baby, two bank robbers drinking coffee, the edge of the volcano, a loose belt, a sorrowful laugh, a broad brushstroke, three dice, the left side of her face, and an orange coat left on a park bench. The gold light hitting the Venetian glass in a way that the heroine could only imagine.

Cast away

there there
now here
where, a solitary pair

swim in separate circles
the water falls into
circular space

cast away
this year and another year
and another year before

on an island, the sand
and the land
where the pair

made a pact
to swim in separate
tides, trunks,

truncation, a vacation,
now here, not here

CROSS-STROKES:

A Reckoning of the Circumambulation
Of West Coast Poetry (1945-2015)

"He who digs Los Angeles IS Los Angeles."
—ALLEN GINSBERG

This anthology was conceived several years ago as a project that would delimit itself by requiring that every poet in it be a resident and working poet in *both* Los Angeles and San Francisco at some point in their lives. The goal was simply to provide readers of contemporary poetry a glimpse at the circulation of poets on the fertile crescent of the West Coast and to disabuse the notion of static, immiscible communities in L.A. and San Francisco. While it remains the case that the majority of poets living in California identify either Los Angeles or San Francisco as an *omphalos* for their poetics, anyone truly familiar with both cities will greet this volume's table of contents as a long forestalled reunion party. Many of these poets not only lived and wrote poems in both cities, but knew each other as friends or at least as friendly comrades in both cities.

Much of the circumambulation, however, was a matter of contingency and happenstance. In taking a close look at the mobility of poets between Los Angeles and San Francisco, one notes how it is almost impossible to predict the journey that any given individual poet might undertake, or how Northern California or Southern California might be lived in more than once in the course of a poet's life. Let us look at a few examples of West Coast tidal fluctuation between L.A. and S.F., working through the table of contents in a chronological fashion.

Bruce Boyd, Stuart Z. Perkoff and John Thomas, for instance, are all poets associated with the Venice West poetry scene, which gained its greatest notoriety due to Lawrence Lipton's best-selling book, *The Holy Barbarians* (1959). Boyd, however, was born in San Francisco and was in the supporting cast of the Berkeley Renaissance. Indeed, it was Jack Spicer who seemed to have gotten Boyd to begin writing poetry in the late 1940s. (Spicer is included in this book to acknowledge his often discounted youth in the Los Angeles area.) By the early 1950s, however, Boyd had moved south, and he was a founding member of the

Venice West scene, as recounted by Perkoff in a long letter to Donald Allen in 1958. Both Boyd and Perkoff appeared in Allen's pathbreaking anthology, *The New American Poetry*, but it should be noted that it was Jack Spicer who first called Donald Allen's attention to Boyd's poetry. Boyd moved back to San Francisco in the late 1950s and then back to Venice in the early 1960s, where he took up residence in the same exact house in Venice that he had lived in before. Boyd did not ever publish a book of poetry and his fate remains even more conjectural than that of Weldon Kees. Nevertheless, he was recognized by his peers, such as Gary Snyder and Stan Perksky, as being a substantial, serious poet.

Both John Thomas and Stuart Z. Perkoff made similar round-trips. Thomas, who was born in 1930, walked out on his wife and children in the late 1950s and began hitchhiking to California. He had not intended to go to Venice, but the perverse luck of the road took him to Southern California. He found himself immediately welcomed into the Venice West community, for in addition to admiring one of their modernist heroes, Ezra Pound, he had the cachet of actually having visited him in St. Elizabeth's. His poem, "The Squirrels," is worth consulting for a masterful pencil sketch of Pound in that troubled confinement. In the early 1960s, as Venice West began to deteriorate both from police surveillance as well as from substance abuse, Thomas moved up to San Francisco, where he wrote some of his best early poems and began to get published in magazines such as *kayak* and *Evergreen Review*. He moved back to Los Angeles in the mid-1960s, and spent the rest of his life here.

Perkoff's round-trip from L.A. to S.F. to L.A. was propelled by more harrowing factors. He was born in St. Louis in 1930, had lived in New York in his late adolescence and early twenties, but then settled in Venice in the early 1950s. In the late 1960s, after getting out of prison, Perkoff moved to Northern California, where he wrote one of his most important long poems, *Alphabet* (Red Hill Press, San Francisco. 1972). Perkoff returned to Venice the year that *Alphabet* was published by Red Hill Press in San Francisco, and he died in Los Angeles in 1974. Finally, as an emphatic rejoinder to those who tend to believe that the movement is always an emigration from Los Angeles to the more poetic climate of the Bay Area, let us not forget William J. Margolis, a World War II veteran who was very active in San Francisco in the 1950s as a poet and editor. Margolis was one of the poets who was closest during that time to Bob Kaufman, the central African-American surrealist of this period. Margolis moved to Los Angeles after suffering a crippling fall and was a member of the Venice West scene in its last stages in the early 1960s.

If Boyd, Thomas, and Perkoff complicate the notion of a one-way ticket between poets who live in Los Angeles and then move north, other poets do confirm that image. David Meltzer as a young, teenage poet visited Venice West, but headed north as soon as possible to become one of the youngest members of the Beat scene as well as the youngest contributors to Donald Allen's anthology.

Lenore Kandel began publishing while she was living in Los Angeles, but once she moved north, she never looked back. In a like manner, Harold Norse spent time in Venice in the early 1960s, though he was never part of the Venice West scene. Once he moved north, he settled in and became one of the established figures in the San Francisco scene.

If Meltzer, Kandel, and Norse headed north to stay, other poets were headed south, though this group tended to have a sense of nostalgia for their points of departure. As with Los Angeles, where the Venice West scene co-existed uneasily with the maverick poets associated with magazines such as *Coastlines*, *Variegation*, and *Trace*, San Francisco also had a plenitude of communities within the alternative it offered American poets. The outskirts of the Bay Area included the small coastal town of Bolinas, which became a magnet for poets from New York starting in the early 1970s. Bolinas proved to be an important way-station, but it was not a final destination for Lewis and Phoebe MacAdams or Aram Saroyan, all of whom have lived in Los Angeles for over a quarter-century. Along with Ellen Sander's similar transplantation from New York to Bolinas to L.A., their move south had been preceded by Kenneth Rexroth's decision to accept a position as a professor at UC Santa Barbara in 1968, where he lived and wrote until his death in 1982.

The year that Rexroth moved to Santa Barbara, Paul Vangelisti also moved south into what he regarded as a permanent exile from his birth-city. His move began in a conventional manner; he enrolled in a Ph.D. program at the University of Southern California, but he left A.B.D. (all but dissertation) to launch a literary magazine (*Invisble City*) and a small press (Red Hill Press) that rank in the very top of such endeavors during that period. Between 1971 and 1982, *Invisible City* published a substantial number of the poets who appear in this anthology. It serves as the single most important meeting place of poets affiliated with both Los Angeles and San Francisco. The *Invisible City* connection between L.A. and S.F. included contributors to that magazine such as Neeli Cherkovski, Jack Hirschman, and Joe Safdie.

Cherkovski was born in Santa Monica and grew up in Los Angeles; while he moved to San Francisco in the mid-1970s, he didn't leave without first publicly identifying himself as a Los Angeles poet. Indeed, the first time I saw Cherkovski's name in print was as a co-editor (along with Paul Vangelisti and Charles Bukowski) of the first of several anthologies to focus on L.A. poetry in the 1970s and 1980s. *Anthology of L.A. Poets* appeared as a thin paperback issued by Red Hill Press in 1972, and both that book and Paul Vangelisti's *Specimen '73* featured the work of Jack Hirschman, who would also permanently relocate from Los Angeles to San Francisco by the mid-1970s. Hirschman's journey along the West Coast has a deeper background story than Cherkovski's in that his influence was felt both on academic premises in Los Angeles and in the counter-culture. In terms of inspiring younger poets in Los Angeles, in fact, Hirschman's presence in both Topanga Canyon and Venice was probably even more important to the poets who were gathering at Beyond Baroque than the Venice West scene. Hirschman embodied a total commitment to poetry that had a seemingly inexhaustible hunger for the renewal of visionary consciousness.

Joe Safdie and Sharon Doubiago probably serve as the most well-traveled contributors to this collections. Both grew up in Los Angeles, but have spent a large portion of their lives living elsewhere. Safdie has lived in Boulder, Colorado; San Francisco; Bolinas; Prague, Czechoslovakia; Seattle, Washington; and the north county of San Diego. Doubiago has undertaken journeys that go the full length of both American hemispheres and published an extraordinary amount of poetry. In embodying her distinct blend of feminist agency in her writing, she epitomizes the restless poetics and thoughtful critique that have grown out of the Beat movement.

In thinking of Joe Safdie's most recent residence on the West Coast, one must take into consideration the role that other cities on the West Coast have played in this complicated game of musical chairs. In particular, two of the most prominent poets living in San Diego, for instance, both have a keen association with Northern California. Rae Armantrout was born and raised in San Diego; though she did attend college there, she ended up matriculating at uc Berkeley and getting a M.A. at San Francisco State University., after which she became a prominent member of the nascent Language school. She returned to Southern California to teach part-time for many years at uc San Diego, where she is now a full professor. One of her colleagues at ucsd is Michael Davidson, who was born in the Bay Area and went on to write a pathbreaking book of literary criticism about the San Francisco Renaissance. Davidson, too, is part of the migratory pattern of West Coast poets that this volume of poetry is meant to illustrate.

Nor is San Diego the only site that represents the distinct north-south oscillation that periodically sends a quiver through the tectonic plates of West Coast poetry. Peter Levitt, for instance, lived in San Francisco briefly after finishing his studies with Robert Creeley at suny Buffalo, and then spent his formative years as a poet in Los Angeles; he was one of only eight poets to appear in both of my anthologies (*The Streets Inside: Ten Los Angeles* and *"Poetry Loves Poetry"* (1985). Levitt lived in Ocean Park, a neighborhood just to the north of Venice, for most of his time in Los Angeles in 1970s, and then lived in Topanga until he moved to Vancouver in Canada in 2000 and became a Canadian citizen. It is not our intention, however, to put together some kind of comprehensive and definitive collection of poetic journey to the far north of the Bay Area or the outliers of Southern California. In many ways, this anthology is but a sketch of a much larger project that I hope someone will take on in the next two decades.

Heading north, also, in the wake of Jack Hirschman and Neeli Cherkovski was Stephen Kessler, a young poet who had studied with Hirschman at ucla and who had ultimately dropped out and headed to Santa Cruz, where he launched *Alcatraz* anthology series. Both as a critic and editor/publisher, Kessler became one of the most adamant supporters of Los Angeles poets such as Wanda

Coleman and Leland Hickman. His contribution to the development of Los Angeles poetry between 1975 and 1985, in fact, is much greater than many of the poets who never left the city.

Also moving to Santa Cruz from Los Angeles at the 1970s/1980s juncture was Nathaniel Mackey, who settled in at UC Santa Cruz as an extremely productive poet. In more recent years, Los Angeles native Doren Robbins made the Santa Cruz area his home, and found that working there has enabled him to retain the cinematic vitality that infuses his imagery. As for other poets moving south, however, in counterpoint, a poet such as Richard Garcia comes to mind. While living in his home town, Garcia had produced one book of youthful poetry that might well be one of the best first books of poetry ever written. Shortly after a letter from Octavio Paz helped Garcia break out of a self-imposed writing block that lasted a decade, Garcia moved to Los Angeles and worked as an artist-in-residence at the Children's Hospital. Like Nathaniel Mackey, he has recently moved out of California, and now lives on the east coast. By now their work has achieved a signature sound that makes its origins on the West Coast felt in every syllable. A fully mature poetics was also present in Michelle T. Clinton's poems when she moved to Berkeley from Los Angeles shortly before her second book from West End Press was published. Anthologized in my *Poetry Loves Poetry*, she went on to claim two appearances in *Best Poems of the Year* after moving north.

Other north and south exchanges involve poets from Long Beach moving north (such as Tim Donnelly, Francisco Alarcon, and Maw Shein Win, all of whom attended CSU Long Beach) and other poets from the Bay Area, such as S.A. Griffin, heading south. As is the case with most of these poets, one would be hard-pressed to bet on their current urban locations being a final node as a look-out point.

Suzanne Lummis and Susan Suntree would also be California poets who have lived in different parts of the state before settling in Los Angeles. Charles Harper Webb lived in Seattle and began publishing poetry while still living there before moving to Los Angeles. All of this is to say that the poets featured in this anthology are meant to serve as representative embodiments of the movement of poets along the West Coast. No one should regard the selection of these particular poets in *Cross-Strokes* as an attempt to anoint them as the central figures of West Coast poetry after World War II. Indeed, such poets as Todd Baron and the late Beat poet John Montgomery may well have a better claim to meeting the original residential and creative paradigm of this anthology than a couple of the poets who made the roster. That said, both Neeli Cherkovski and I believe that the variety of poets in this collection is emblematic of shifts within important microcosms of American poetry that have yet to be fully recognized by canonical authorities on the east coast. The canon is yielding, however; one poet who would certainly deserve to be in any subsequent version of this anthology, Juan Felipe Herrera, has just been appointed the next Poet Laureate of the United States.

Many of the poems in this collection owe a significant debt to the Beat poets, but one last poet remains to be considered as a counterweight to their practice. Standard Schaeffer had the good fortune to come of age in Los Angeles at a time when the work done by Paul Vangelisti, Martha Ronk, Bob Crosson, and Dennis Phillips, as well as the late Leland Hickman, began to take hold as a model for an alternative to the mass-produced anecdotal poetry that seemed to exert its charms with surprising ease in the final decades of the twentieth century. Schaeffer eventually moved to San Francisco and then to Portland, which recently had a significant anthology of its poets. One contributor to that volume was Carol Ellis, who lived and wrote in the Los Angeles area for many years. At every instance, one must adjust the mirrors to show the larger patterns of West Coast fermentation.

Finally, there is the case of Tim Reynolds, who had extraordinary success as a young poet who caught the attention of Kenneth Rexroth and who then traveled the world until finally settling in Los Angeles in the early 1980s. Within the context of this company of poets, it is appropriate that his brief memoir, *Whatever Happened*, was published by Brooks Roddan's If Publications before Roddan moved north to San Francisco at the beginning of this decade. Roddan is a recent example of the northern migration, and has a more than legitimate claim as a poet to being in this book, but since he was also my publisher while living in Los Angeles, I felt there was a potential conflict of interest.

The most knowledgeable readers of contemporary poetry will notice a number of significant omissions, which I cannot explain in any other terms but the chance shuffling of various lists the editors composed over the five years this project was in the making. Certainly poets such as Leslie Woolf Hedley, Alfred Arteaga, Steve Carey, F.A. Nettlebeck, and William Oandasan are superbly eligible and worthy of inclusion in this anthology.

Whatever else might be said about the peregrinations of all these poets, one must concede that no other comparable pattern can be found in the United States. There is no indication, for instance, that a substantial number of early- to mid-career poets move so freely between Boston and New York, or Philadelphia and Washington, D.C. While both Los Angeles and San Francisco possess a radiant charisma distinctive unto themselves, the West Coast is even more powerful in exerting its subtle wanderlust along its shores. No other region seems to make use of the antinomian spirit that continues to revivify American poetry at its best. Whatever contumacious magic this concept still possesses, it can be found hard at work in the on-going renaissance of California's provisional directories of contemporary poets.

Bill Mohr
California State University, Long Beach
billmohrpoet.com

Other Titles from Otis Books | Seismicity Editions

Erik Anderson, *The Poetics of Trespass*
  Published 2010 | 112 pages | $12.95
  ISBN-13: 978-0-979-6177-7-5
  ISBN-10: 0-979-6166-7-4

J. Reuben Appelman, *Make Loneliness*
  Published 2008 | 84 pages | $12.95
  ISBN-13: 978-0-9796177-0-6
  ISBN-10: 0-9796177-0-7

Bruce Bégout, *Common Place. The American Motel*
  Published 2010 | 143 pages | $12.95
  ISBN-13: 978-0-979-6177-8-2
  ISBN-10: 0-979-6177-8-

Guy Bennett, *Self-Evident Poems*
  Published 2011 | 96 pages | $12.95
  ISBN-13: 978-0-9845289-0-5
  ISBN-10: 0-9845289-0-3

Guy Bennett and Béatrice Mousli, Editors, *Seeing Los Angeles:*
A Different Look at a Different City
  Published 2007 | 202 pages | $12.95
  ISBN-13: 978-0-9755924-9-6
  ISBN-10: 0-9755924-9-1

Robert Crosson, *Signs/ & Signals: The Daybooks of Robert Crosson*
  Edited by Guy Bennett and Paul Vangelisti,
  with an Introduction by Guy Bennett
  Published 2008 | 245 pages | $14.95
  ISBN: 978-0-9796177-3-7
  Co published with The Archive for New Poetry,
  Mandeville Special Collections Library,
  University of California, San Diego

Robert Crosson, *Daybook (1983–86)*
  Published 2011 | 96 pages | $12.95
  ISBN-13: 978-0-9845289-1-2
  ISBN- 0-9845289-1-1

Mohammed Dib, *Tlemcen or Places of Writing*
  Translated from the French by Guy Bennett
  Published 2012 | 120 pages | $12.95
  ISBN-13: 978-0-9845289-7-4
  ISBN-10: 0-9845289-7-0

Ray DiPalma, *The Ancient Use of Stone: Journals and Daybooks, 1998–2008*
  Published 2009 | 216 pages | $14.95
  ISBN: 978-0-9796177-5-1

Ray DiPalma, *Obedient Laughter*
   Published 2014 | 144 pages | $12.95
   ISBN: 978-0-9860173-3-9

Jean-Michel Espitallier, *Espitallier's Theorem*
   Translated from the French by Guy Bennett
   Published 2003 | 137 pages | $12.95
   ISBN: 0-9755924-2-4

Forrest Gander, Editor, *Panic Cure: Poems from Spain for the 21ˢᵗ Century*
   Translated from the Spanish by Forrest Gander,
   with an Introduction by Daniel Aguirre-Orteiza
   Published 2014 | 304 pages | $12.95
   ISBN-13: 978-0-9860173-4-6
   ISBN: 0-9860173-4-5

Leland Hickman, *Tiresias: The Collected Poems of Leland Hickman*
   Edited by Stephen Motika, with a Preface by Dennis Phillips
   and an Afterword by Bill Mohr
   Published 2009 | 205 pages | $14.95
   ISBN: 978-0-9822645-1-5
   Co-published with Nightboat Books

Norman M. Klein, *Freud in Coney Island and Other Tales*
   Published 2006 | 104 pages | $12.95
   ISBN: 0-9755924-6-7

Michael Joyce, *Twentieth Century Man*
   Published 2014 | 152 pages | $12.95
   ISBN: 987-0-9860173-2-2

Luxorius, *Opera Omnia or, a Duet for Sitar and Trombone*
   Translated from the Latin by Art Beck
   Published 2012 | 216 pages | $12.95
   ISBN-13: 978-0-9845289-6-7
   ISBN-10: 0-9845289-5-4

Ken McCullough, *Left Hand*
   Published 2004 | 191 pages | $12.95
   ISBN: 0-9755924-1-6

Béatrice Mousli, Editor, *Review of Two Worlds: French and American Poetry in Translation*
   Published 2005 | 148 pages | $12.95
   ISBN: 0-9755924-3-2

Laura Mullen, *Enduring Freedom*
   Published 2012 | 80 pages | $12.95
   ISBN-13: 978-0-9845289-8-1
   ISBN-10: 0-9845289-8-9

Ryan Murphy, *Down with the Ship*
   Published 2006 | 66 pages | $12.95
   ISBN: 0-9755924-5-9

Aldo Palazzeschi, *The Arsonist*
    Translated from the Italian by Nicholas Benson
        Published 2013 | 232 pages | $12.95
        ISBN: 978-0-9845289-9-8

Dennis Phillips, *Navigation: Selected Poems, 1985–2010*
        Published 2011 | 288 pages | $14.95
        ISBN-13: 978-0-9845289-4-3
        ISBN: 0-9845289-4-6

Antonio Porta, *Piercing the Page: Selected Poems 1958–1989*
    Edited, and with an Introducction by Gian Maria Annovi,
    with an essay by Umberto Eco
        Published 2011 | 368 pages | $14.95
        ISBN-13: 978-0-9845289-5-0
        ISBN: 0-9845289-5-4

Eric Priestley, *For Keeps*
        Published 2009 | 264 pages | $12.95
        ISBN: 978-0-979-6177-4-4

Sophie Rachmuhl, *A Higher Form of Politics: the Rise of a Poetry Scene, Los Angeles, 1950-1990*
    Translated from the French by Mindy Menjou &
    George Drury Smith
        Published 2014 | 352 pages | $12.95
        ISBN-13: 978-0-9860173-5-3
        ISBN-10: 0-9860173-5-3

Olivia Rosenthal, *We're Not Here to Disappear*
    Translated from the French by Béatrice Mousli
        Published 2015 | 176 pages | $12.95
        ISBN-13: 978-0-9860173-7-7
        ISBN-10: 0-9860173-7-x

Ari Samsky, *The Capricious Critic*
        Published 2010 | 240 pages | $12.95
        ISBN-13: 978-0-979-177-6-8
        ISBN-10: 0-979-6177-6-6

Hélène Sanguinetti, *Hence This Cradle*
Translated from the French by Ann Cefola
        Published 2007 | 160 pages | $12.95
        ISBN: 970-0-9755924-7-2

Giovanna Sandri, *only fragments found: selected poems, 1969–1998*
    Edited by Guy Bennett, with an Introduction by Giulia Niccolai
    Translated from the Italian by Guy Bennett, Faust Pauluzzi,
    and Giovanna Sandri
        Published 2014 | 336 pages | $14.95
        ISBN-13: 978-0-9860173-1-5
        ISBN-10: 0-9860173-1-0

Janet Sarbanes, *Army of One*
    Published 2008 | 173 pages | $12.95
    ISBN-13: 978-0-9796177-1-3
    ISBN-10: 0-9796177-1-5

Severo Sarduy, *Beach Birds*
    Translated from the Spanish by Suzanne Jill Levine and Carol Maier
    Published 2007 | 182 pages | $12.95
    ISBN: 978-9755924-8-9

Adriano Spatola, *The Porthole*
    Translated from the Italian by Brendan W. Hennessey and
    Guy Bennett, with an Afterword by Guy Bennett
    Published 2011 | 112 pages | $12.95
    ISBN-13: 978-0-9796177-9-9
    ISBN-10: 0-9796177-9-0

Adriano Spatola, *Toward Total Poetry*
    Translated from the Italian by Brendan W. Hennessey and
    Guy Bennett, with an Introduction by Guy Bennett
    Published 2008 | 176 pages | $12.95
    ISBN-13: 978-0-9796177-2-0
    ISBN-10: 0-9796177-3-1

Carol Treadwell, *Spots and Trouble Spots*
    Published 2004 | 176 pages | $12.95
    ISBN: 0-9755924-0-8

Paul Vangelisti, *Wholly Falsetto with People Dancing*
    Published 2013 | 136 pages | $12.95
    ISBN-13: 978-0-980173-0-8
    ISBN: 0-9860173-0-2

Allyssa Wolf, *Vaudeville*
    Published 2006 | 82 pages | $12.95
    ISBN: 0-9755924-4-0a